Jw 96-23-42 &c FM 18-5

WAR DEPARTMENT

TANK DESTROYER
FIELD MANUAL

*

ORGANIZATION AND TACTICS
OF TANK DESTROYER UNITS

June 16, 1942

FM 18–5

TANK DESTROYER FIELD MANUAL

ORGANIZATION AND TACTICS OF TANK DESTROYER UNITS

UNITED STATES
GOVERNMENT PRINTING OFFICE
WASHINGTON : 1942

WAR DEPARTMENT,
WASHINGTON, June 16, 1942.

FM 18–5, Tank Destroyer Field Manual, Organization and Tactics of Tank Destroyer Units, is published for the information and guidance of all concerned.

[A. G. 062.11 (5–26–42).]

BY ORDER OF THE SECRETARY OF WAR:

G. C. MARSHALL,
Chief of Staff.

OFFICIAL:

J. A. ULIO,
Major General,
The Adjutant General.

DISTRIBUTION:
Bn and H 1–7, 17, 18 (3) ; I C 2–7, 9–11 (3) ; C 17, 18 (20).
(For explanation of symbols see FM 21–6.)

TABLE OF CONTENTS

FOREWORD

This manual contains doctrines for the training and combat employment of tank destroyer battalions and groups. It is prepared for the guidance of units that will be equipped with matériel now being developed; units equipped with substitute matériel must interpret and modify the provisions of this manual to fit their particular needs. Furthermore, methods of application must be adapted to the particular terrain and climatic conditions of the various theaters of operation.

There is but one battle objective of tank destroyer units, this being plainly inferred by their designation. It is the destruction of hostile tanks. Throughout all phases of training and during preparation for combat, this objective will be kept in mind by all ranks. The attainment of this objective demands: (1) the selection of individuals of a high mental and physical type for assignment to tank destroyer units; (2) the attaining and maintaining of top physical condition; (3) the perfection of all phases of technical training to such an extent that the interchange of duties of any tank destroyer team will not detract from its effectiveness; (4) the inculcation of courageous but intelligent aggressiveness, the willingness to assume responsibility in the absence of orders, and the exercise of initiative and forethought in making instantaneous decisions to meet any change in any situation.

TANK DESTROYER FIELD MANUAL

ORGANIZATION AND TACTICS OF TANK DESTROYER UNITS

CHAPTER 1

ARMORED COMBAT

SECTION I

CHARACTERISTICS OF ARMORED FORCES

■ 1. NATURE OF ARMORED COMBAT.—*a*. The combat employment of tank destroyer units against armored forces demands of all ranks a comprehensive knowledge of the capabilities of tanks and of tank tactics. This chapter presents portions of this necessary knowledge. Further detailed information will be found in FM 17–10, FM 17–20, TM 30–450, and TM 30–480.

b. Armored combat is characterized by great mobility, fire power, armor protection, and shock action. Primarily offensive in character, this highly mobile warfare is conducted by powerful self-sustained units composed of specially equipped troops of the necessary arms and services, acting in close cooperation with combat aviation and other ground troops.

■ 2. ARMORED FORCES.—*a*. Armored forces consist of motorized combat vehicles of various types, tank elements, and such appropriate elements of the arms and services as are required to form a balanced combat team. Large armored forces, such as divisions and corps, are capable of dealing with most combat situations. Special task forces combining suitable proportions of the different arms with armored forces are formed for the accomplishment of special missions.

b. Armored forces are primarily organized, trained, and equipped for offensive operations against vital objectives deep in the hostile rear. They aim at the quick seizure of critical

1

areas, the destruction of rear installations, and the prevention of movements by reserves. Their objectives may be reached by envelopments, penetrations, or turning movements.

c. Armored forces are particularly well suited to conduct a pursuit.

d. The conditions which should exist or be created for their successful action are air superiority in the decisive area of employment, surprise, favorable terrain, and the absence or neutralization of massed defensive means.

e. The reconnaissance element of an armored force provides the commander with the necessary information upon which his plan of action is based. It is composed of a large proportion of lightly armored vehicles, well equipped with radio, and smaller elements of light tanks, artillery, engineers, and infantry. Occasionally medium tanks are included. Motorcycles are used for messenger service, marking of routes, and traffic control. Observation aviation closely cooperates with the reconnaissance echelon.

f. The tank echelon of an armored force is its most powerful unit; it provides its main striking force. The success of a tank attack, once launched, depends upon the neutralization of the enemy antitank defenses. All arms support the attack to this end.

g. The infantry echelon of an armored force directly aids tank units in capturing ground initially denied to tank operations by enemy antitank installations. It attacks antitank guns. It drives enemy covering forces from defended tank obstacles, thus permitting their removal or destruction. It assists in the exploitation of a penetration. Infantry takes over, consolidates, and holds ground gained by tank operations. It protects the reorganization of tank units.

h. The artillery echelon of an armored force gives timely maximum fire support to the tank attack. Mobile armored forward observation posts are often utilized to observe fire. A portion of the artillery, equipped with armored self-propelled mounts, accompanies the tank attack. This assault artillery, using direct laying, seeks to neutralize located hostile antitank guns.

i. Combat aviation prepares and supports the tank attack

by demoralizing ground forces, neutralizing antitank guns, and by preventing the movement of reserve units.

j. Engineer units of the armored force assist the advance and attack of the tank echelon by the removal and reduction of artificial obstacles and by the preparation of crossings over natural obstacles.

■ 3. CHARACTERISTICS OF ARMORED FORCE MATÉRIEL.—*a*. *Tanks*.—(1) The tank is the backbone of armored forces. These powerful, track-laying, automotive vehicles possess great fire power, both in small arms automatic weapons and in cannon; are capable of speeds of from 25 to 50 miles per hour on good roads; and may move in large masses cross country at speeds of 15 miles per hour and more. Tanks possess the ability to overrun and crush matériel and emplacements.

(2) The accuracy of fire delivered from moving tanks is considerably less than that of stationary firing.

(3) The mobility of tanks is materially effected by terrain and climatic conditions. Fog, dust, and smoke will retard speeds, particularly when it is necessary to drive with ports closed. Mud, heavy snow, marshy ground, large obstacles, dense woods, and various types of artificial installations will slow down operations. Extremely hot weather is very enervating to tank personnel; extremely low temperatures cause great difficulty in mechanical operation.

(4) All tanks are designed to give the maximum armored protection to the front of the vehicle. Heavy armor usually is not used on the sides and rear in order to avoid excessive weight. Sloping armor gives much greater protection than surfaces which permit normal impact of armor-piercing ammunition; it is difficult to obtain sloping surfaces along the sides of the tank. These conditions render most tanks far more vulnerable to fire delivered from the flank or from the rear.

(5) Tracks, drive sprockets, vision slits, periscopes, gun ports, the belly, and the junction of the turret with the hull of the tank are all more or less vulnerable to the effect of fire.

b. Armored cars.—These vehicles form a large proportion of reconnaissance elements; they are used as personnel and ammunition carriers, as command vehicles, and as armored mobile artillery observation posts. Armored cars also are used as self-propelled mounts for light caliber antitank and antiaircraft weapons. They may be armed with caliber .30 or heavier machine guns and may carry radio equipment.

c. Half-track vehicles.—Half-track vehicles combine some of the advantages of track-laying vehicles with those of wheeled vehicles. Road speeds up to 45 miles an hour are feasible, and cross country mobility is very good. This type of vehicle is contained in several different armies; its uses range from carrying personnel to providing mounts for medium artillery.

SECTION II

TANK TACTICS

■ 4. GENERAL.—Tanks attain their greatest power when employed in mass. All echelons of the armored force give all possible assistance to the attack of its main striking force, the tank element.

■ 5. SURPRISE.—The greatest adjunct to successful tank attack is surprise, gained through secrecy, rapid maneuver, or deception. Tanks initially may be held in concealed positions, well back from the area of combat, and brought to assault positions under cover of darkness. When conditions are favorable, the movement from rear areas may be made in daylight hours and conducted at maximum speed. The attack is then launched with a minimum of delay, so as to strike before hostile forces have opportunity to readjust their dispositions.

■ 6. ATTACK.—*a. General.*—(1) Objectives of tank attacks are usually deep in the hostile rear; in moving on such objectives, tanks seek to avoid engagement against strongly organized defenses. When required to break through hostile dispositions, their attack is massed initially on a narrow front; it is extended promptly in width and depth when exploitation is begun following penetration of the hostile position. "Soft spot" tactics characterize tank action during the attack; leading elements often pass by defended localities, leaving them to be reduced later by other troops which attack from flank and rear.

4

(2) Prior to launching an attack, strong reconnaissance elements feel out hostile dispositions to locate weak points; the main attack is usually concentrated against one of these.

(3) The time and direction of a tank attack may be based upon climatic conditions. Attack at dawn, or early daylight, is favored when a secret night movement to a concealed assault position can be effected. In desert warfare great advantage is gained in attacking from the direction of the sun, early or late in the day. Except when attacking with infantry or in very open terrain, tanks are likely to use some feature to maintain direction. Tank attacks are often directed with a main road as the axis.

(4) In massed attacks against organized resistance, tanks usually attack in two or three echelons. The first echelon may be charged with rapidly overrunning the antitank guns and artillery of the defense and then exploiting. The second may follow the first to extend or deepen exploitation; in some cases it may be employed to help the infantry overcome hostile defenses. The third echelon usually constitutes a reserve; elements assist at times in mopping-up operations.

(5) Tank attacks are assisted by air action and the fire of infantry and artillery weapons. Special attention is usually given the flanks of the attack, which are protected by powerful concentrations. The use of smoke is likely in rear areas.

b. *Fire and movement.*—Attacking tanks advance by a combination of fire and movement. The leading waves are charged with the destruction of located antitank weapons. Throughout all echelons overwatching tanks cover by fire the advance of maneuvering tanks. Located antitank weapons are subjected to fire from tanks in the leading wave, from covering tanks, and from assault artillery which follows the attack closely. Fire of tanks against antitank guns will often be from machine guns rather than cannon; it is usually easier to destroy the crew than the gun. Tanks coming under fire of antitank weapons may either move quickly to hull defiladed positions and open fire from a stationary position, or if cover is not available, move toward the gun with the purpose of overrunning it. Smoke may be used to blind the antitank gun.

c. Contact.—Contact with friendly units operating on the enemy flanks is disregarded, the tank attack being pushed as hard and as fast as possible.

d. Exploitation.—When the rear of the hostile position has been gained, attacking tanks fan out and proceed to disrupt lines of communication and supply, to destroy artillery positions, command posts, and communication centers, and to overrun reserves.

e. Reorganization.—Control of large masses of tanks, once an attack has been launched, is extremely difficult. Brief halts for reorganization and refueling may be necessary; at such times tanks are extremely vulnerable. Infantry and tank destroyer units following the attack protect tank units during this period.

■ 7. VARIATIONS IN TANK TACTICS.—While the foregoing indicates the general nature of tank action, experience during the current war has clearly indicated the fallacy of preconceived convictions as to the employment of tanks. Novel and unexpected methods have been completely successful in many instances. Commanders who have based their actions upon the belief that hostile tanks would attack in a commonplace, orthodox manner have frequently met disaster.

■ 8. OBSTACLES.—In both Belgium and France in 1940, German tank units broke through very heavy artificial obstacles and forced river crossings rapidly. In the Balkans in 1941, difficult mountain passes were negotiated by German tanks in spite of strong resistance. In Malaya in 1942, Japanese tankettes achieved surprise by crossing flooded rice fields that were believed to be impassable. The placing of undue reliance on passive protection afforded by large streams, dense woods, and other natural and artificial obstacles has frequently proved to be a fatal error.

CHAPTER 2

TANK DESTROYER CHARACTERISTICS AND ORGANIZATION

SECTION I

MISSION AND CHARACTERISTICS

■ 9. ROLE.—*a.* Tank destroyer units are especially designed for offensive action against hostile armored forces. They are capable of semi-independent action but preferably operate in close cooperation with friendly units of all arms. They are allocated to large units as indicated in paragraph 36.

b. When supported units are engaged in offensive action, tank destroyers protect them against armored counterattack and thus allow full exploitation of their success.

c. When a supported unit is engaged in defensive action, a minimum of antitank weapons are located to cover obstacles and establish a first echelon of defense disposed in depth against tanks while a maximum of mobile antitank weapons are held in reserve, prepared for immediate offensive action. Organic antitank weapons of front line units are used for this first line of defense; tank destroyer units form the mobile reserve.

■ 10. CHARACTERISTICS.—*a.* The characteristics of tank destroyer units are mobility and a high degree of armor-piercing fire power, combined with light armor protection; strong defensive capacity against attacks of combat aviation; and flexibility of action permitted by generous endowment with means of communication. Tank destroyer units are also capable of effective action against tanks through the use of close combat weapons.

b. Action of tank destroyer units is characterized by rapid movements, sudden changes in the situation, and a succession

7

of brief but extremely violent combats separated by sporadic lulls. Aggressive fighting spirit and individual initiative are marked features.

c. Highly effective against tanks, tank destroyers are ill suited to close combat against strong forces of hostile foot troops.

■ 11. MISSION.—a. As indicated by their name, the primary mission of tank destroyer units is the destruction of hostile tanks.

b. When tank destroyer units can be spared from this primary mission, they may be employed on secondary missions, such as beach defense, action against parachute and air-borne troops, and the reduction of bunkers, pill boxes, and other weapon emplacements. The decision to employ tank destroyer units on other than primary missions is a responsibility of higher commanders.

SECTION II

MORAL QUALITIES

■ 12. TANK DESTROYER SPIRIT.—Tanks and armored cars can be destroyed only by tough and determined fighting men who are masters of their weapons. Tank destroyer soldiers are taught that they must be superior soldiers. The moral qualities of aggressiveness, group spirit, and pride in an arduous and dangerous combat mission must pervade each tank destroyer unit. All ranks must possess a high sense of duty, an outstanding degree of discipline, a feeling of mutual loyalty and confidence with regard to their comrades and leaders, and a conscious pride in their organization.

■ 13. LEADERSHIP.—The tank destroyer spirit can be developed only through the highest type of leadership. Detailed discussion of this military requisite is found in FM 100-5. The encouragement of initiative is a salient feature of leadership in tank destroyer units.

SECTION III

WEAPONS

■ 14. SELF-PROPELLED MOUNTS.—a. *Types of weapons.*—The primary weapons of tank destroyer units are self-propelled guns with high velocities and flat trajectory. These vehicles provide limited armor protection to crews and can move into and out of firing position rapidly. The guns are of several different calibers.

(1) *37-mm gun.*—The general characteristics of this weapon are given in FM 23–70. It is capable of effective action against the majority of tanks at ranges of 500 yards or closer and against light tanks and armored cars at greater ranges. Its fire must be directed against the more vulnerable portions of heavily armored tanks. Several hits may be required to knock out such vehicles. Its projectile loses penetrating power rapidly as the impact varies widely from normal. Its high mobility, rapidity of fire, ease of concealment, and the light weight of its ammunition fit this weapon particularly for delaying, harassing, and security missions and for action against hostile armored reconnaissance elements and light tanks.

(2) *75-mm gun.*—The general characteristics are given in TM 9–305. Using armor-piercing ammunition, this cannon is effective against most tanks at ranges up to 1,000 yards. The heavy impact of the projectile may disable a tank at greater ranges without necessarily penetrating its armor. This is particularly true of hits on the tracks, drive sprockets, and on the turret.

(3) *57-mm gun.*—This weapon has slightly greater penetrating power than the 75-mm gun and is capable of destroying most tanks at ranges of 1,000 yards or greater.

(4) *3-inch antitank gun.*—This weapon when firing armor-piercing ammunition has tremendous tank destructive powers. A single projectile will usually disable any tank that is solidly struck at ranges up to 2,500 yards.

b. Types of ammunition.—All armor-piercing ammunition for the weapons listed above carry a visible tracing compound in the base of the projectile. This greatly facilitates the adjustment of fire on moving targets. A small proportion of high explosive ammunition for use against personnel is usually carried with these weapons. The high explosive ammunition of 3-inch guns is effective against tanks as well as personnel. If armor-piercing projectiles for the 75-mm gun are lacking, unfuzed shell should be fired against tanks;

otherwise smoke of the first explosion may obscure the target.

c. Methods of fire control.—Direct laying is habitually employed by tank destroyer guns. Under exceptional circumstances, such as the definite location of a large mass of tanks at long range, the heavier calibered weapons may employ simple methods of indirect laying, the fire being adjusted by an observer in a forward armored mobile observation post. High explosive ammunition will be used. Ammunition to be expended under these circumstances must be made available by the supported unit; weapons must always retain adequate ammunition for their principal method of action against tanks.

■ 15. TOWED GUNS.—Tank destroyer units may be equipped with towed guns of the same characteristics as those just described. Towed guns can be easily and quickly concealed but require considerably more time to get into and out of position. Improvised methods of porteeing towed guns may give them some of the desirable characteristics of self-propelled guns.

■ 16. AUXILIARY WEAPONS.—The following auxiliary weapons greatly augment the effectiveness of tank destroyer units:

a. Antitank grenades.—The most powerful offensive adjuncts to the antitank guns of tank destroyer units are antitank grenades. These powerful short range weapons provide crews of self-propelled weapons with an effective means of combating and destroying tanks at close range if their primary weapon or its vehicle is disabled. They render every small reconnaissance and security detachment a dangerous menace to tanks. (See FM 23–30.)

b. Antiaircraft weapons.—Caliber .50 machine guns on suitable mounts provide antiaircraft protection against low-flying combat aviation and dive bombers. When not required for antiaircraft protection, they are used for augmenting destroyer fire against tanks.

c. Mines.—A limited number of mines is carried by tank destroyer units to block corridors or favorable tank approaches not covered by gun fire, for close protection of gun positions, for use in ambushes, and to canalize the advance of tanks into areas that are covered by gun fire. The quantities carried are not sufficient to permit the laying of a large mine field. Promiscuous use of mines risks being as dangerous to friendly as to hostile troops; exceptional precautions are required in their employment. (See FM 100–5.)

   d. *Smoke-projecting devices.*—Each combat vehicle carries a small number of hand smoke grenades and smoke pots. Smoke placed as a screen in front of destroyers neutralizes the accuracy of hostile fire, and permits unobserved maneuver. Even greater protection against fire results when the smoke is placed on the hostile tank or weapon. Tanks are blinded in passing through smoke, direction is frequently lost, speed of maneuver decreases, and if the immediate terrain is full of obstacles such as stumps, large trees, ditches, or streams, they may be immobilized. In addition to this, tanks emerging from a smoke cloud are sharply silhouetted against the white background and present an excellent target.

   e. *Individual weapons.*—All personnel are armed with the pistol, the rifle, or the carbine for individual protection. In addition hand grenades are carried on each combat vehicle.

Section IV

COMMUNICATIONS

■ 17. GENERAL.—*a.* The critical importance of time in tank destroyer operations, particularly during actual combat, demands that every possible method of rapid communication be employed. Two-way radio, both voice and code, is the principal method used, but complete reliance cannot be placed on this for all phases of operation. Additional means of communication include messengers (airplane, motor, motorcycle, and foot), visual signals (pyrotechnics, flashlights, flags, panels, and airplanes), liaison officers, and, in exceptional cases, telephones.

   b. At all times, commanders should be prepared to utilize emergency communication in the event the enemy jams frequencies assigned to tank destroyer units and to the warning system. Plans for emergency use should include the utilization of all possible methods.

■ 18. RADIO COMMUNICATION.—*a.* Two-way radio communication is provided for within the battalion down to and including platoon leaders. Certain section leaders are provided with receivers.   Two-way cleared channels are allocated to battalions by higher headquarters for command and anti-tank warning service. (See ch. 11.)

b. The large number of sets in the battalion requires rigid net control and discipline, in addition to thorough training in operation and maintenance of all sets.

c. When in contact with the enemy, voice radio messages from platoons and companies, in principle, will be transmitted by officers.   The officer is the combat operator and directs his unit, microphone in hand.   During this period the regularly assigned operator keeps the set in operation, properly tuned, and receives and sends messages in the absence of the officer to whom the set is assigned.   In the unusual case when it is impracticable for the officer to act as combat operator, he writes out messages for transmission or dictates them phrase by phrase while remaining near the operator.   In the latter case he listens to the transmission and instantly corrects errors.   The officer is responsible for all errors and omissions.

d. Information of the enemy at times may be sent in the clear, but identifications of friendly troops, their location, operation, and movement are usually disguised by suitable simple codes. Destroyer unit commanders in transmitting orders and instructions by radio endeavor to use language understandable to the units receiving them but meaningless to the enemy.   In addition to the prescribed brevity and map coordinate codes, destroyer battalion and company commanders may select identified terrain features in the zone of combat and designate them as reference points.   Battalion reference points are lettered; those of the companies are numbered. Selection of more than two or three reference points by each unit is inadvisable. Mention of such reference points can be made over the air without divulging information to the enemy. Reference points will not be *identified* over the radio. Details of codes are covered in signal operation instructions of the particular unit. Provisions must be included in the preparation of such codes to permit their being quickly changed. Codes must be changed daily or more often during active operations.

e. Radio silence should not be imposed upon active reconnaissance detachments of tank destroyer battalions when combat is imminent.

■ **19. ARM-AND-HAND SIGNALS.**—*a*. Drill and combat arm-and-hand signals applicable to tank destroyer units are described in FM 18–15.

b. A few additional visual signals using colored flags, disks, blinkers (flashlights), and colored smoke may be used for the tactical control of small units. Attempts to employ a large number of signals usually lead to confusion. Such signals are included in the signal operation instructions (SOI) of the particular unit.

■ **20. PYROTECHNICS.**—Very pistols and ground projectors are furnished tank destroyer units. Due precautions must be taken to insure that the use of these signals will not confuse friendly troops with which tank destroyer units may be associated.

■ **21. AIR-GROUND PANELS.**—*a*. Air-ground liaison panels are used to supplement, and if necessary to substitute for, the usual radio communication with observation aviation. (See FM 24–5.)

b. In addition to these panels, plainly recognizable identification panels should be provided for battalion headquarters, and all observation aviation operating with the tank destroyer units informed in advance of their design. Small panels are of little value. The panel should be at least as large as the body of a tank destroyer, and should be of a color that can be easily seen.

c. In emergencies an airplane may communicate with ground troops by simple maneuvers of the plane while in flight. Any code devised should be prescribed in signal operation instructions.

■ **22. MESSENGERS.**—Motorcycle or motor messengers may be used to assist in clearing radio traffic, or when radio silence is in effect. They are used to deliver marked maps and sketches. Motorcycles are preferable if messenger routes are crowded with traffic. Motors (¼-ton trucks) have much better speed in mud, sand, or cross country travel. Small units may use foot messengers when other means fail. When available, air-borne messengers provide the means for rapid transmission of important messages.

■ 23. LIAISON OFFICERS.—Liaison officers are habitually used by tank destroyer battalions attached to large units, to insure that close contact with the commander is maintained. A liaison officer will always be sent to the headquarters of the supported unit. Often it will be advantageous to send a liaison officer to the headquarters of the reconnaissance unit of the supported organization. They are transported in organic vehicles equipped with two-way radio. If part of a tank destroyer group, a battalion sends a liaison officer to the group commander. (See par. 164.)

■ 24. TELEPHONES.—Telephones, without wire, are, carried in the battalion for use with higher headquarters. The higher unit furnishes wire if telephones are to be used. When operating in friendly territory, these telephones permit utilization of commercial wire lines, if available, and may be advantageously used to tie in with antitank warning service installations.

■ 25. MAPS AND MESSAGES.—The use of simple maps, overlays, and sketches for dependable transmission of information assists in maintaining communication at the efficient peak required in tank destroyer operations.

SECTION V

GENERAL ORGANIZATION

■ 26. GENERAL.—*a.* The semi-independent nature of tank destroyer operations requires that tank destroyer units be self-contained. Personnel, equipment, and training of tank destroyer units conform to this necessity.

b. Tank destroyer units will be subject to alterations; changes of weapons, equipment, and details of organization may be frequent. Moreover, the exact amounts and types of prescribed equipment may not always be available. Tank destroyer commanders must develop the capacity to handle groupings which are formed as task forces.

■ 27. TANK DESTROYER BATTALION.—The tank destroyer battalion is the basic tactical unit for operation against enemy

14

armored elements in conjunction with, or in support of, infantry, cavalry, motorized, and armored divisions. The battalion consists of a headquarters and headquarters company, three tank destroyer companies, and a reconnaissance company. For details of organization and equipment, see T/O 18–25.

■ 28. HEADQUARTERS AND HEADQUARTERS COMPANY.—*a.* Command, staff, administrative, personnel, motor maintenance and inspection, and supply echelons of the battalion are grouped in the headquarters company. For details of organization and equipment, see T/O 18–26.

b. This organization operates to free the combat companies from administrative and supply burdens. Kitchen, combat, gas and oil, ammunition trucks, and heavy maintenance vehicles are pooled. If companies are detached from the battalion, the necessary supply vehicles will accompany them.

■ 29. TANK DESTROYER COMPANY.—*a.* The tank destroyer companies of the battalion, the main fighting element, are composed of a headquarters, one light destroyer platoon, and two heavy destroyer platoons. For details of organization and equipment, see T/O 18–27.

b. To insure that destroyers are given protection against hostile ground and air forces, security and antiaircraft elements are included in destroyer companies.

■ 30. RECONNAISSANCE COMPANY.—The reconnaissance company is the principal information-gathering agency of the battalion. It consists of a headquarters, three reconnaissance platoons, and a pioneer platoon. For details of organization and equipment, see T/O 18–28.

■ 31. TANK DESTROYER GROUPS.—Tank destroyer groups are organized for operations against large armored forces. Their composition may vary materially. The main striking force of the group consists of tank destroyer battalions. Other elements are attached in accordance with the mission of the group and the situation. The tank destroyer group is controlled, supplied, and administered by a headquarters and headquarters company organized in accordance with T/O 18–10–1.

CHAPTER 3

COMBAT

SECTION I

DUTIES OF COMMANDERS

■ **32. GENERAL.**—Tank destroyer commanders meet their responsibilities by intelligent anticipation, timely decisions, plans and orders, and supervision of execution. Haste in execution cannot make up for time lost through lack of planning. The necessary preparations for combat, including reconnaissance, the formulation and issue of orders, the movement of troops into assembly areas or positions in readiness, and arrangements for supply and communication, so far as possible are carried on concurrently. Warning orders permit subordinates to make timely preparations in anticipation of final orders. Rapidity of maneuver is not attained by neglecting essential steps in the organization of combat action.

■ **33. ESTIMATE OF SITUATION.**—A tank destroyer commander engages his unit according to a definite plan based upon an estimate of the situation. (See FM 101–5.) During active operations, this estimate is constantly being formulated and revised in accordance with the latest information of the enemy, the situation of the unit, the terrain in its vicinity, and other pertinent factors. A tank destroyer commander must always be prepared to commit his unit to prompt action.

■ **34. PERSONAL RECONNAISSANCE.**—The personal reconnaissance of a tank destroyer commander must be executed rapidly; usually little time will be available because of the speed with which tank destroyer units operate. Before starting he should know where he is going, what he is looking for, the time available, and the route to be taken. Aimless reconnaissance without specific purpose or direction is usually of slight value.

16

■ **35. ORDERS.**—*a.* Simplicity, brevity, and rapidity of issue and distribution characterize orders in tank destroyer units. Formal written orders are exceptional. The order initiating an operation should be as complete as the situation permits; subsequent instructions usually consist of brief fragmentary orders and messages, usually transmitted by radio.

b. When the utmost speed is required, a few words transmitted by radio are used to assign initial combat missions. Frequently this is done in a brevity code. At times the order may consist merely of a code word directing execution of a prearranged maneuver.

c. Transmission of oral orders may be facilitated in the preliminaries of battle by the assembly of subordinates to receive instructions; during combat such procedure is seldom 'practicable or advisable.

d. When time permits oral orders are issued methodically. Notes prepared by a commander insure that no essential item is omitted. An operations map or sketch issued to subordinates just prior to issuance of the order often facilitates understanding of information and instructions. When not pressed for time, the commander, before commencing his order, thoroughly orients his subordinates on the ground or on the map or sketch. Having completed the orientation, the commander commences the oral order, speaking slowly enough to permit the taking of notes. He frames his order as nearly as practicable with the same directness, brevity, and sequence as observed in written orders. He excludes details which are not essential to the mission of subordinates and which burden their memory and attention. Having completed the order, the commander invites questions, and answers them with patience and thoroughness. When mutual understanding is complete, watches are synchronized. The subordinate who receives an oral order records as much of it as is necessary under the circumstances. Brief notes and marks on a map or sketch usually suffice.

e. A complete combat order may contain the following:

(1) (*a*) *Enemy information.*—Emphasize the latest identifications of tanks and aircraft and reports of movements of tanks and other armored vehicles.

(*b*) *Information of our own and supporting troops.*—Loca-

17

tion and proposed employment of friendly troops. Identification of friendly tanks operating in the vicinity. Missions and locations of nearby antitank weapons, and of adjacent and supporting units. Locations of mines and natural and artificial obstacles.

(2) *Mission of unit.*—Indicate the objective, or the troops, installations, or terrain feature to be protected. Include such of the following as are required: time and direction of advance; zone of action; dispositions; limit of pursuit; route; time of departure; order of march for movement into initial positions.

(3) (a) *Mission of subordinate elements.*—Assign to each its combat task indicating such of the following as are necessary: objective; initial position; direction of movement; combat area; primary, alternate, and supplementary positions; sectors of fire; special reconnaissance or security missions; instructions regarding contact with friendly troops.

(b) *Miscellaneous.*—Indicate conditions under which fire is to be opened, rallying position, and alternate rallying position.

(4) *Administrative details.*—Arrangements for ammunition, fuel, and rations; location of aid stations or nearby medical establishments; instructions for maintenance elements.

(5) *Details regarding communications.*—Warning service; location of command post; prearranged signals; instructions regarding the use of radio.

f. Each tank destroyer commander passes on promptly to his subordinates fragmentary orders or information concerning the foregoing items when it is impracticable for him to issue a combined order.

g. For further data in regard to combat orders, see FM 101-5.

Section II

ALLOCATION AND EMPLOYMENT OF UNITS

■ 36. Tactical Allocation.—*a.* The allocation of tank destroyer units to subdivisions of a major force will vary with circumstances. Factors that must be considered for such allocations are—

(1) Mission of the major force, and its subdivisions.

(2) Means available to the opposing forces, particularly the strength in armored elements.

(3) Conditions in the theater of operations, including terrain.

(4) Probable and possible future action.

b. In general, sufficient tank destroyer strength to meet their usual needs is distributed among divisions, while much stronger forces are assigned to higher units. A typical allocation might be—

(1) With each infantry, cavalry, armored, or motorized division: one tank destroyer battalion.

(2) With each army corps: one or more tank destroyer groups, each consisting of three or more tank destroyer battalions and reinforcing elements of the arms and services.

(3) With each field army: several similar groups.

(4) Under the theater commander awaiting assignment to task forces or allotment to armies: several groups.

This allocation facilitates the rapid massing of tank destroyer units as demanded by the situation and lends itself to the expeditious forming of special task forces as their need develops. It presents increasingly powerful resistance to the progress of any hostile attack.

c. The employment of the tank destroyer units is included in the general plan of action of the force to which they are allocated. Initially tank destroyer units are usually held in concealed positions far enough to the rear to permit employment anywhere over a wide zone of action. They are moved, preferably under cover of darkness, to the area selected for their engagement as the situation develops.

■ 37. EMPLOYMENT.—Tank destroyer units are employed offensively in large numbers, by rapid maneuver, and by surprise.

■ 38. OFFENSIVE ACTION.—Offensive action allows the entire strength of a tank destroyer unit to be engaged against the enemy. For individual tank destroyers, offensive action consists of vigorous reconnaissance to locate hostile tanks and movement to advantageous positions from which to attack the enemy by fire. Tank destroyers avoid "slugging matches" with tanks, but compensate for their light armor and difficulty of concealment by exploitation of their mobility and superior observation.

19

■ 39. MASS.—The employment of tank destroyer units will be in mass. The battalion is the smallest unit which should be engaged separately. Employment of small tank destroyer units as independent defensive elements and their distribution with a view to covering every possible avenue of tank approach or to affording immediate protection to all echelons of the forces leads to uncoordinated action and dispersion with consequent loss of effectiveness.

■ 40. MANEUVER.—a. Rapidity of maneuver enables tank destroyer units to strike at vital objectives, fight on selected terrain, exercise pressure from varied and unexpected directions, and bring massed fire to bear in decisive areas. Tank destroyer units obtain results from rapidity and flexibility of action rather than by building up strongly organized positions. Tank destroyers depend for protection not on armor, but on speed and the use of cover and terrain. When maneuvering in the presence of the enemy they habitually move at the greatest speed permitted by the terrain.

b. Rapidity of maneuver of large tank destroyer units is attained as much through thoroughness of anticipatory planning and reconnaissance and the efficient functioning of communications as through the inherent speed of tank destroyer vehicles.

c. Effective use of tank destroyer mobility is predicated upon road priorities, use of reserved roads, and effective cooperation by military police in the combat zone. As in the case of a fire department, the way must be cleared for tank destroyers when the time for action arrives.

■ 41. SURPRISE.—a. Tank destroyer units attain surprise by concealment of the time and place of their action, screening of dispositions, rapidity of maneuver, deception, and occasional adoption of unorthodox procedure.

b. Decoying the enemy into ambushes is characteristic of tank destroyer tactics. Attacks with the sun in the eyes of the enemy favor surprise and marksmanship.

■ 42. FIRE AND MOVEMENT.—a. Tank destroyers act by a combination of fire and movement to reduce hostile opposition. Movement of maneuvering elements is protected by the fire of other elements in position. The purpose of the maneuver is to gain positions that permit still more effective fire on the enemy. At the same time movement serves to protect tank destroyers from hostile fire. This method of attack is applicable to all elements of tank destroyer forces.

b. The fire from the primary gun of a moving tank destroyer is inaccurate. The tank destroyer halts and fires from suitable positions. Duration of occupation of any one position is brief. Obtaining a hit on the first shot is of critical importance. Fire is as rapid as accuracy permits.

■ **43. TERRAIN.—***a.* The employment of tank destroyer units must be based on a careful study of the ground. Commanders of larger tank destroyer units plan their maneuver so as to act on chosen ground. The terrain selected should afford ample maneuver room to permit full advantage to be taken of the mobility of their vehicles.

b. Advance in the presence of the enemy must be conducted so as to avoid encountering the enemy while on unfavorable terrain or in unsuitable dispositions.

■ **44. INITIATIVE.—***a.* The rapid developments of mechanized combat require maximum initiative on the part of all tank destroyer personnel. Commanders will often be confronted with the problem of making an immediate decision and initiating prompt action. Decisions made should be in general conformity with the intentions of the commander; it is essential, therefore, that all be informed of those intentions.

b. In the absence of orders and when consistent with their mission, tank destroyer units sent into areas where tanks do not appear assist adjacent units which are engaged, or seek tanks reported in nearby areas. Their action is reported at the earliest opportunity. (See par. 85*a.*)

■ **45. SIMPLICITY.—**Diversity of tank destroyer armament and the rapidity with which units must operate require assignment of definite functions to varied elements to expedite and simplify tactical operations. Familiarity of a unit with a limited number of relatively definite tactical procedures permits it to meet the majority of situations advantageously without excluding modification appropriate to the particular situation.

21

■ 46. SECURITY.—Regardless of security measures provided by other troops, tank destroyer units habitually provide all-around security for themselves against both ground and air forces.

■ 47. WARNING SERVICE.—The efficient operation of a tank warning service which transmits rapidly to tank destroyer commanders information as to the strength, location, and direction of movement of hostile tanks is essential. (See ch. 11.)

■ 48. RECONNAISSANCE.—*a.* Due to the large areas involved in tank destroyer operations, reconnaissance begins early and is continuous and extensive. Reconnaissance by tank destroyer personnel is primarily intended to insure the advantageous entry into battle and effective combat action of their own unit. Alternate plans of action, based on reconnaissance, provide for movement to and occupation of concealed initial positions, corresponding to each plan.

b. Great economy of reconnaissance personnel must be exercised in the earlier stages of operations. The main reconnaissance effort for tank destroyer units will always be made during combat and while tank destroyer units are advancing to contact, in order to permit the tank destroyer commander to make suitable dispositions for the movement of his command and for its engagement. Sufficient reconnaissance forces must be held in hand for this emergency and not prematurely dissipated. The assistance of observation aviation during this period is of the greatest importance.

■ 49. ELASTICITY.—Methods of employment of tank destroyer units must be highly elastic and will vary to meet and counter the tank tactics of hostile forces.

■ 50. DECENTRALIZATION.—Combat action of tank destroyer units is characterized by decentralization. Responsibility for combat tasks is fixed by assignment of simple missions in accomplishing which the subordinate has great freedom of action. Frequent alterations of original missions or assignments of entirely new tasks are to be expected.

■ 51. DEPTH.—Tank destroyer units, down to and including companies, usually hold out a reserve initially to exploit advantages gained in the first contacts or to meet flanking or encircling action of attacking tank units. Platoons are usually disposed in depth with rear elements covering the flanks of more advanced elements.

■ 52. FRONTAGES.—*a.* The methods of tank destroyer employment do not require rigid assignment of areas or frontages; where such assignment is made, it usually contemplates initial or temporary occupation only.

b. Where tank destroyer units are assigned, through necessity, large areas of frontages for occupation, such areas or frontages are held by holding a unit under control in a central location or by leaving gaps between subordinate elements, rather than by extending the usual intervals between guns. Cordon dispositions are avoided. When engaged against a powerful opponent, a company will not usually occupy an area wider than 1000 yards. In contact operations against small forces, such concentration is not essential.

■ 53. AVOIDANCE OF ALINEMENT.—Tank destroyer units make no attempt to maintain alinement with adjacent tank destroyer or other units. Provision is made to protect exposed flanks; contact with adjacent units may be maintained by patrols. Disposition of small groups in wedge or clusters facilitates readiness for action and adaptation to the terrain.

■ 54. COOPERATION OF OTHER TROOPS.—Employment of tank destroyer units should be in close coordination with other troops. Calls for the assistance of other troops are made without hesitation when tank destroyers are confronted with situations with which they are not designed to cope. Maximum combat aviation support is particularly essential in fast-moving situations. Actions and dispositions of anti-tank units, artillery, and antiaircraft artillery strongly influence tank destroyer employment.

■ 55. ATTACKS ON TANKS IN ASSEMBLY AREAS.—*a.* When hostile tank forces are known to be assembled within striking distance, tank destroyer units with the necessary reinforcements may make incursions within the hostile lines to strike at them. Opportunities most frequently result when the vicissitudes of combat create numerous salients and reentrants along the general front of contact. Such surprise attacks on

23

tanks in bivouac or assembly positions are best accomplished late in the day or in early morning.

b. A blow at a large tank force sheltered behind hostile dispositions usually requires the action of a strong task force of all arms, including tank destroyer units, and involves a decision by higher commanders.

■ 56. RECOVERY SYSTEM.—Automatic functioning of a recovery system whereby disabled tank destroyers are promptly repaired on the battlefield is an important factor in maintaining the combat efficiency of units. During lulls in combat, tank destroyer commanders cause damaged vehicles to be towed to the nearest areas offering cover, where repair operations are initiated without delay. (See FM 18-10.)

SECTION III

POSITIONS AND AREAS

■ 57. GENERAL.—Certain areas or positions utilized in tank destroyer combat are as follows:

Park.
Intermediate position and position in readiness.
Assembly position.
Fire position.
Cover position.
Rallying position.
Combat area.

Qualities which are desirable in most positions are ease of entry and egress, concealment from ground and air, defilade from hostile fire, space to allow sufficient dispersion, remoteness from areas likely to attract enemy fire such as cross roads and artillery positions, protection by natural or artificial obstacles, suitability for local defense, and shelter for personnel and maintenance activities. All-weather hard standings are desirable in all positions and necessary in the base park. Each of the above mentioned areas or positions is briefly discussed below.

a. Park.—A tank destroyer park is a locality in which a unit concentrates or from which it operates. During combat, personnel and matériel not actually engaged remain at the park, and administrative, supply, and maintenance services operate therefrom. The park should be beyond the effective range of enemy artillery.

b. Intermediate position.—An intermediate position between the park and the combat area may be utilized for the temporary halting and concealment of destroyers when required by the tactical or logistical situation (to approach a probable zone of employment during hours of darkness or to cross a defile). An intermediate position may also serve as a position in readiness. A position in readiness is a centrally located area where destroyers are concealed, alert to move quickly to meet a hostile threat. Everything possible to insure timely employment of destroyers is accomplished in advance, to include selection of routes to probable combat areas and, in some cases, selection of positions.

c. Assembly position.—An assembly position is one occupied by an organization preliminary to action against the enemy, for the distribution of orders and other final preparations before entering a combat area. The assembly position also is used for regaining control after interruption of a march. The assembly position should be as close to the expected point of contact as the situation will permit. At times units may move directly from positions in readiness to combat without entering an assembly area.

d. Fire position.—Fire positions are occupied by destroyers in action to cover by fire an assigned sector or avenue of approach. Fire positions are primary, alternate, or supplementary. The primary fire position is the position from which a unit or weapon executes its primary mission. An alternate fire position is a position from which the same fire missions can be executed as from the primary fire position. A supplementary fire position is a fire position from which a destroyer can accomplish fire missions other than those to be accomplished from primary or alternate positions.

e. Cover position.—A cover position is one in the immediate vicinity of the fire position providing concealment and protection to weapons and crew. The cover position is used when adequate cover cannot be had at the fire position. The destroyer remains in the cover position until action is imminent, when it is quickly shifted to the fire position.

25

f. Rallying position.—A rallying position is a place, designated in advance by a unit commander, where he assembles his unit for further operations after an engagement. An alternate rallying position is a place, also designated in advance, where units assemble in case they are unable to reach the rallying position. The alternate rallying position is usually farther to the rear than the rallying position.

g. Combat area.—An area assigned to a destroyer unit within which it is to operate against hostile tanks.

CHAPTER 4

TANK DESTROYER COMPANY

SECTION I

TANK DESTROYER SQUAD AND SECTION

■ 58. TANK DESTROYER SQUAD.—*a. Composition.*—The tank destroyer squad consists of a destroyer commander, a driver, a gunner who lays the piece, and one or more assistant gunners. The commander of one of the two destroyers of a section is also the section leader. When a heavy gun squad consists of only four men, the destroyer commander, in addition to exercising command, assists in the service of the piece.

b. Equipment and transportation.—The tank destroyer squad is transported on a self-propelled antitank gun mount.

c. Fuel and ammunition.—The tank destroyer squad carries sufficient fuel for one day of operation and approximately 50 rounds of heavy or 100 rounds of light ammunition.

■ 59. DESTROYER COMMANDER.—*a.* He is responsible for the conduct of the training of his squad and the care and condition of all individual and squad armament and equipment. He receives and executes orders of the section leader, usually transmitted by voice or visual signals. He sees that lookouts are posted at all times to observe for hostile aircraft or ground troops.

b. On the march he is responsible that the driver and the designated assistant driver perform the proper vehicle checks and that they rotate at the controls so that neither becomes excessively fatigued. He sees that the duties of air sentinel are rotated frequently. He checks equipment for its presence and serviceability and insures that it is located in its proper place and securely fastened. He sees that the driver main-

27

tains proper distance, speed, and road position. He keeps oriented as to the location of the vehicle. He watches the preceding vehicle for signals or changes of direction. At the halt he directs disposition of the vehicle, taking advantage of cover and concealment, or gains security through dispersion. Except in the presence of the enemy, crew members are permitted to relax in order that they may be in condition to take their turn at the above duties. On forced marches the destroyer commander encourages crew members who are not on duty to sleep. During night marches he prevents unnecessary use of unshielded lights and is particularly careful to keep lights from being flashed in the eyes of vehicle drivers. When contact with the enemy appears imminent, without awaiting directions from the section or platoon leader, he orders the crew to take action posts and load the piece. After preparing for action he will frequently check to see that all members are observing their sectors and are prepared for action.

c. In combat, subject to limitations imposed by orders of the section leader, he reconnoiters, selects, occupies, and improves the destroyer position and directs the action of the crew. (See FM 18-15.) He frequently checks on the sight adjustment by bore-sighting; this is particularly important following movement of a destroyer. In case a disabled destroyer is in danger of capture, the destroyer commander insures its destruction.

d. During lulls in combat, and upon arrival in an assembly or rallying position, he informs the section leader concerning casualties, ammunition, and fuel supply.

■ 60. DRIVER.—In bivouac he is responsible for camouflaging the destroyer. He keeps it headed out and prepared for prompt movement without necessity of backing. On the march he keeps a sharp lookout for mines and obstacles. He looks for routes offering cover and defilade, and watches the vehicle ahead for signals. In combat he observes to the front, reports menacing targets promptly to the destroyer commander, and is ready to maneuver the destroyer to meet them. During actual firing he watches the traverse of the piece and, upon signal of the gunner, is ready to move instantly when the gun reaches the limit of traverse. He studies the ground, and is prepared for any possible move that he may be directed to make. Before commencement of a combat action, he empties the extra fuel that is carried on the vehicle into the fuel tank or otherwise disposes of it. He keeps the destroyer commander informed concerning the supply of gas and oil and any other matters pertaining to the operation of the vehicle. He is responsible for first echelon maintenance of the vehicle and for making motor maintenance inspections as prescribed in FM 18–15.

■ 61. GUNNERS.—While on the march in the combat zone, the gunners keep a constant lookout for hostile ground or air forces. When the destroyer is in cover or firing positions, they observe in assigned sectors. In action, they take maximum advantage of their armored protection while performing crew functions. They assist in the care and maintenance of the destroyer and all weapons and equipment and operate secondary armament, as directed by the destroyer commander.

■ 62. TACTICS.—a. General.—In combat the destroyer is either in a firing or cover position, or moving from one position to another. The time required for a move from one position to another and the exposure during the move are reduced by reconnaissance and the selection of routes and new positions before the destroyer moves out from the old position. Adequate reconnaissance will save time and prevent undue exposure through false moves to positions which prove unsatisfactory.

b. Reconnaissance of position.—The destroyer commander determines the best route into and out of his assigned area and selects within that area the most advantageous position or positions from which to accomplish his mission. When time permits, this reconnaissance is made on foot. Since this often will not be feasible, the destroyer commander and every member of the crew must constantly consider two vital questions:

(1) Where is the next suitable firing position—to my front—to my flanks?

(2) What is the best available route to that position—out of the position?

Every time a hill is crossed or a corner turned, these questions must be asked and answered.

c. *Selection of positions.*—The primary consideration is that the destroyer must be suitably located to accomplish its mission of timely and effective fire on any part of its sector. Extensive use is made of cover positions. When a cover position is selected, the destroyer commander reconnoiters, preferably on foot and accompanied by one or more gunners, and marks the location of the firing position. When a man of average height can see the target or assigned sector over the top of a crest while standing, this position is usually suitable for a destroyer firing position. In selecting routes and positions the destroyer commander endeavors to comply with the following basic guides:

(1) Take advantage of concealment when moving into position; avoid movements over or along a crest which will present a clear silhouette to the enemy.

(2) Do not wait for orders when the enemy launches a surprise attack, but move off the road at once to the nearest position and open fire.

(3) Select positions from which movement can be made without delay to the front or rear.

(4) In any firing position, seek concealment and hasty camouflage. Avoid firing positions on a hill crest; seek a position that provides partial defilade, and which has an irregular background.

(5) Select firing positions with unrestricted fields of fire, and that do not offer covered approaches to the enemy.

(6) Exploit difficult terrain and natural obstacles to the advantage of the destroyer and the disadvantage of the enemy.

d. *Occupation and improvement of position.*—Tank destroyer units occupy selected positions rapidly, by covered routes and without unnecessary lateral movement. A destroyer commander begins improving his position as soon as it is occupied. Alternate and supplementary positions, both cover and firing, are selected and routes to them are reconnoitered.

e. *Fire mission.*—A tank destroyer squad is normally given a specific fire mission including a primary sector of fire. When required by the situation, the squad fires in other sectors. The conditions for opening fire must be clearly understood. Fire may be withheld for a radio or other pre-arranged signal given by the section, platoon, and, at times, company commander. Specific orders governing the opening of fire will often be given with respect to visible terrain features. In the absence of instructions or in emergencies, the destroyer commander determines when to open fire.

f. Conduct of fire.—(1) Opening of fire is governed by many factors, including the number of hostile vehicles which are exposed, the degree of concealment afforded the destroyer, proximity of cover into which target vehicles might vanish, the effective range of the destroyer against the target in question, the extent to which the terrain favors machine gun fire by a moving tank, and the mission of the destroyer in question.

(2) Fire will not be opened at ranges that are likely to be ineffective. Premature opening of fire gives warning and discloses positions. Against small numbers of tanks, well-concealed destroyers seldom open fire at ranges greater than 500 yards. Destroyers with a skirmishing or delaying mission may open fire at longer ranges. When large numbers of tanks expose themselves in a mass attack, opening fire at effective ranges will be normal. In flat, treeless areas where concealment and, hence, surprise fire is difficult, fire is opened at the longest range promising remunerative results.

(3) Once fire has been opened, any tank within effective range is engaged. The crews of moving tanks are relatively deaf and blind. These handicaps should be exploited by the use of ambush wherever possible. For example, three tanks which appear to be traveling a course that will take them to the flank of a gun position should be permitted to come almost abreast of the position and the *last* tank in the column engaged first, then the second in column, and last, the first in column.

(4) On the other hand, when tanks approach and threaten a gun position, the tank which is most menacing (usually the closest to the gun) should be fired upon until hit; then the next nearest (or most menacing) should be fired upon. It must be noted, however, that the most effective fire from tank guns is obtained when firing from a halted tank.

31

Consequently, a halted tank that is firing upon the gun posi-. tion may be more menacing than a closer, moving tank.

(5) Whenever practicable, tanks which are covering the advance of other tanks by firing from a stationary position in hull defilade should be neutralized by smoke while maneuvering tanks are being engaged.

(6) So far as practicable, destroyers seek to deliver fire against the sides of a tank or to strike it at a normal angle of impact. As soon as a tank has been stopped, it is usually advisable to fire one or more additional shots to insure its destruction and prevent it from opening effective fire from a stationary position. In case appearance of an emergency target prevents such action, the destroyer disables the immobilized tank at the earliest opportunity.

(7) After firing three or four rounds, the destroyer changes position unless a remunerative target is in sight, in which case it continues to fire but changes position at the first opportunity. Displacement to the alternate position is by a previously selected route.

(8) The destroyer commander exercises care to insure that his squad is in constant readiness to meet attacks of successive elements of enemy tanks.

(9) If the vehicle has to retire across open ground, use of smoke to mask hostile observation is advisable.

■ 63. TANK DESTROYER SECTION.—a. Composition.—The tank destroyer section is composed of two tank destroyer squads. It is commanded by a sergeant who is also leader of one of the squads.

b. Communication.—The section may receive orders from the platoon leader by radio. Communication between the destroyers of a section is maintained by voice, visual signals, or messenger.

c. Duties of personnel.—The duties of individuals are as listed in paragraphs 59, 60, and 61. The section leader has additional duties as listed below:

(1) He transmits and has executed all orders and instructions of the platoon leader. He is responsible for the training of the section and the care, cleaning, and operation of its equipment and armament. He usually operates the radio.

(2) On the march he leads his section and performs the duties listed in paragraph 59 with respect to his own destroyer.

He supervises the duties of the squad leader of the other destroyer in his section. While marching in the combat zone, the section leader constantly studies the terrain, and is prepared to commit his destroyers to prompt action. If the section is acting independently and advancing by bounds, the section leader's destroyer will always be the leading element. The section leader regulates the advance by use of signals. In case of a sudden attack while on the march, he signals ACTION LEFT (RIGHT, FRONT), and by his action and signals indicates the action for the other destroyer.

(3) At halts he conducts such inspection of matériel and equipment as is necessary. In bivouac he locates his destroyers as directed by the platoon leader and supervises the execution of all instructions concerning camouflage, digging of slit trenches, and other special security measures. He reports to the platoon leader when his destroyers are cleaned, serviced, filled with gasoline, and ready for movement, or he indicates items that he cannot correct.

(4) In combat he regulates the action of the section in accordance with the orders of the platoon leader or the requirements of the situation.

d. *Hasty selection and occupation of position.*—When sudden action is ordered, the section leader, without halting for further reconnaissance, signals ACTION, and points in the desired direction. He then halts his destroyer in the nearest suitable firing position. He readjusts dispositions as opportunity permits.

e. *Deliberate selection and occupation of position.*—(1) In situations where time is ample, a more detailed reconnaissance, selection, and occupation of position are made. Sections may be halted under cover (destroyers pointing out ready to fire) while the section leader and assistant, on foot, reconnoiter the assigned fire position area, for routes and positions, with the following in mind:

(a) Upon terrain which tends to canalize the direction of tank approach, and which affords some natural protection to the position area, effort is made to obtain enfilade fire.

(b) An ambush position requires complete concealment for destroyers and personnel. Cover positions are usual.

(c) Destroyers will be mutually supporting. They should not be placed so far apart that control by voice, signal, or

33

messenger is lost. However, they should be separated by at least 50 yards.

(2) Based upon this reconnaissance the section leader assigns a position or position area to the other destroyer of his section and issues the necessary instructions for its occupation. These instructions will include—

> Primary sector of fire.
> Time for opening fire.
> Plans for next displacement.
> Location of section leader's destroyer.

f. Organization of position.—After the occupation of the position, the section leader, as soon as possible—

(1) Ascertains the areas which security elements near his section are guarding and observing. He assigns at least one man to be on the alert for signals from these security groups.

(2) Sees that destroyer crews use all available time for camouflage and for improving the local defenses of the position area by the use of natural obstacles, augmented in some cases by artificial obstacles. They may prepare slit trenches near the destroyer if the position is to be occupied for a considerable period.

(3) Transmits additional instructions of the platoon leader as soon as received.

g. Combat action.—Destroyers in cover positions move into firing positions upon signal of section leaders or observers. During the fire fight, communication between destroyers may be impractical. The second destroyer conforms, in general, to the action of the section leader's destroyer. If an extensive change of position is necessitated, the section leader at first opportunity reestablishes communication with the platoon leader and reports the change in dispositions. When the section has opened fire and disclosed its position, the section leader, at the first opportunity, displaces the section to alternate fire positions. Usually one destroyer will move at a time, covered by the fire of the other. In the absence of orders, or if time is not available to contact the platoon leader, the section leader takes such action as will best further the combat mission of the platoon. He does not hesitate to move his section to forestall attempts at flanking action by hostile tanks. As opportunity arises, he reestablishes communication with the platoon. At the earliest opportunity after combat, the section leader will report to the platoon leader on the condition of his section. Primary items included in this report are—

> Casualties.
> Fuel and ammunition.
> Damage to vehicles or weapons.

The section leader causes gun crews to be reorganized and redistributes ammunition if necessary.

h. Local security.—When providing local security of a bivouac or position by covering a road, destroyers are placed in positions away from the road but permitting effective fire on the road. The destroyers are mutually supporting and may have the same primary fire mission. They are usually given local protection by security elements, posted in slit trenches.

SECTION II

ANTIAIRCRAFT SECTION

■ 64. COMPOSITION AND DUTIES.—This section consists of two multiple antiaircraft weapons on self-propelled mounts, and personnel and equipment as prescribed in T/O 18–27. The antiaircraft section leader also acts as gun commander of one of the weapons. Duties of individuals on the march, at halts, and in bivouac correspond in general to those prescribed for the tank destroyer squad (pars. 59, 60, and 61). Personnel of the section are thoroughly trained in the technique of fire against ground targets in addition to antiaircraft fire applicable to their particular weapons.

■ 65. MISSION.—The primary mission of the section is to protect the platoon from air attack. Its secondary mission is action against hostile tanks.

■ 66. DISPOSITION.—*a. In bivouac and assembly areas.*—In bivouac or in assembly areas, antiaircraft sections will be posted so as to provide coordinated all-around air defense. Air sentinels are provided during daylight hours and sufficient personnel remain in the immediate vicinity of the guns to insure that they are manned in case of alarm.

b. On march.—The antiaircraft section marches as a unit

behind the rear tank destroyer section on night marches and when hostile air attack is improbable. When air attack is anticipated, the section leader's vehicle moves immediately in rear of the first tank destroyer section and the other antiaircraft gun follows the second tank destroyer section.

c. In combat.—(1) In combat the antiaircraft section will usually be placed in rear of the tank destroyer platoon where it can obtain concealment and still have an adequate field of fire. Distance behind tank destroyer sections will depend on the terrain and the armament with which the antiaircraft section is equipped. If practicable, antiaircraft guns will be posted close enough to each other to facilitate control by the section leader; however, this consideration must be subordinated to effective protection of tank destroyer sections. Antiaircraft weapons must remain in the vicinity of tank destroyer sections (distance not normally exceeding 200 yards). Each antiaircraft gun is normally affiliated with a given tank destroyer section and unless the platoon leader directs otherwise an antiaircraft gun is posted generally in rear of the tank destroyer section so as to protect it against dive-bombing attacks or flanking action by hostile tanks. In case a tank destroyer section moves several hundred yards from its original position, the affiliated antiaircraft group automatically acompanies it unless otherwise directed. The antiaircraft group usually does not displace when destroyers effect only minor changes of position.

(2) During the engagement the platoon leader may call upon the antiaircraft section to cover either or both flanks to stop an encircling maneuver by hostile tanks. In selecting positions, routes over which antiaircraft weapons may be moved to fulfill this secondary mission are given consideration. The range at which antiaircraft weapons are effective against tanks is also a factor.

(3) In exceptional circumstances, the antiaircraft section may reinforce security groups against infiltration by hostile ground troops.

■ 67. AMMUNITION SUPPLY.—If air activity is intense, supply of ammunition to the antiaircraft guns will present difficulties. The platoon leader may give priority to the needs of antiaircraft guns and keep the platoon ammunition vehicle in their vicinity.

SECTION III

SECURITY SECTION

■ 68. COMPOSITION.—The composition and equipment of the security section are listed in T/O 18–27. It is divided into groups, each with its own transport. One group is commanded by the sergeant and the other by the corporal.

■ 69. MISSION.—The primary mission of the security section is to protect the platoon against hostile foot troops and to provide warning of tank attacks. Secondary missions include the attack of tanks, employment as reconnaissance patrols, furnishing guides and route markers, and protecting the leader's reconnaissance parties.

■ 70. DUTIES.—The duties of the personnel of the security section on the march, at halts, and in bivouac in general correspond to those listed for the tank destroyer squad. (See pars. 59, 60, and 61.)

■ 71. TRAINING.—For basic training of the security section, see FM 21–45 and FM 21–100. For technique of fire in combat, see appropriate Field Manuals for weapons in question. The security section is especially trained in methods of destroying tanks by the use of grenades and mines. It is trained in combat and terrain reconnaissance.

■ 72. OUTGUARDS.—In bivouac, mutually supporting elements of security sections will be posted to provide local security and to protect destroyers and antiaircraft weapons. Security section groups also may be employed as patrols and outguards at some distance from the bivouac. For details, see FM 21–100.

■ 73. ON THE MARCH.—On the march the security section normally moves as a unit directly behind the platoon leader, and is available for combat, security, or reconnaissance missions to the front or flanks. When the platoon halts temporarily, members of the security section establish local security, dismounting and moving to nearby points of observation. At longer halts it may form part of a more elaborate march outpost. Dispositions favor a rapid assembly so as not to delay the platoon in moving out.

■ 74. ADVANCE GUARD POINT.—*a*. When the platoon acts as advance guard, one group of the security section, assisted by one or more motorcycle scouts from company headquarters, acts as point. The point is both a reconnaissance and security element. It usually precedes the rest of the platoon by about 1 minute (600 yards). The point advances rapidly along the road until indications of the presence of the enemy are received. In close proximity to the enemy, the advance is conducted by bounds. On winding roads, or where visibility is limited, elements within the point are particularly careful to maintain visual contact until the next bound is reached.

b. The point reconnoiters the road on which the column is marching and observes to the immediate flanks. It remains on or near the route of advance. It gives timely warning to the platoon leader of the enemy's presence or of road blocks, mines, or other obstructions. It removes small obstacles from the route. It pushes boldly into villages along the line of march to determine whether or not they are occupied by the enemy. It drives back or disperses small hostile patrols. When the enemy encountered is too strong to be defeated by the point, it protects and warns the next element in the rear.

c. The point commander gives the necessary orders to the point and insures that the designated route is followed. In case it becomes impracticable, or obstacles are encountered, he notifies the platoon leader and reconnoiters for routes around the obstacle. In case the enemy opens fire on the point, he reports contact and sends members of the point to reconnoiter the enemy position, to fire on and mark the hostile flanks with tracer ammunition, and to signal if the enemy withdraws. As soon as practicable he informs the platoon leader of the hostile strength, composition, and dispositions. If the scouts sent out from the point remain out of view for an unreasonable period, he assumes that they have been shot or captured and sends dismounted scouts to reconnoiter the place where they disappeared.

d. In the execution of its mission, elements of the point proceed as follows: Two vehicles work as a pair, making successive bounds at the maximum speed which road conditions permit. The point commander is in the second vehicle. At the end of each succeeding bound the leading vehicle slows down, halts short of the crest, bend, etc., and observers dismount and move to reconnoiter the terrain to the front and check the route. The crew of the second vehicle observe to the flanks. The motorcyclist is employed in a position where he can observe for at least 600 yards. The leading vehicle does not move forward to the next bound until it has signaled "Forward." Control is maintained by visual signals. (See FM 18–15.) When an obstacle or enemy is discovered, one man reports this to the point commander; the others remain in observation. When fired upon, the crew of the leading vehicle seek cover, report contact, and then reconnoiter to determine the direction and nature of the hostile action. They fire their weapons in self-defense and to warn elements in rear. In case fire is opened on troops in rear from a hostile position which has been passed without being observed by the crew of the leading vehicle, it will return, dismount, and attack the enemy. It will especially seek to bring under fire antitank guns and machine guns.

■ 75. COVERING ACTION.—When the platoon is effecting a deployed advance in the presence of enemy mechanized forces, the security section may advance by bounds on a broadened front to successive commanding terrain objectives. Movement is on vehicles. Each bound of movement is directed upon a terrain line of importance to the security of the platoon or to its eventual combat action. The security group, upon reaching an objective, deploys to screen the employment of destroyers or prepares to continue their advance in accordance with orders or signals.

■ 76. GUARDING PLATOON LEADER.—One group of the security section accompanies the platoon leader when he moves forward on reconnaissance. If the group is in two vehicles, one vehicle remains near the platoon leader while the other precedes him and reconnoiters the area into which he is about to move.

■ 77. SCREENING ASSEMBLY AREA.—During the occupation of an assembly area, rallying position, or platoon cover position, the security section dismounts and provides a local screen of security and observation. The distance of observers from the platoon depends on the terrain; it will rarely be more than 100 or 200 yards.

■ **78. COMBAT ACTION.**—*a.* In combat the security section usually protects the flanks of the platoon. Positions of groups will preferably be such that they can fire across the front of the platoon against any enemy advancing from that direction and at the same time block avenues of hostile approach from the flanks. When the platoon moves into combat, the security section, unless otherwise ordered, splits into groups, one group being affiliated with each tank destroyer section. In the absence of other orders, the group remains in support of its tank destroyer section, and *its combat employment will be based upon the action of that section.* The security group leader is responsible for ascertaining the position of destroyers and maintaining contact with the tank destroyer section. The security group accompanies or precedes the destroyers on all major displacements, covering them when practicable. For limited displacements security units move dismounted, with their vehicles following by bounds. Security section drivers endeavor to keep their vehicles in a defiladed position centrally located with respect to the position of security groups. The vehicle should be within at least 200 yards of the crew and preferably closer. When the tank destroyer section is in a firing position, the affiliated security group usually places observers well forward on the exterior flank of the section to give warning of the approach of hostile mechanized units and to guard against infiltration of hostile infantry. The entire security section may be employed on an exposed flank.

b. During combat the security groups take advantage of all opportunities to attack tanks whenever their action is not required against hostile foot troops. In particular, tanks which attempt to bypass destroyer positions my moving through wooded areas are particularly vulnerable to attack by small patrols from the security section. Movement through woods requires exposure of tank personnel while the woods reduce the speed of the tank movement and enable attacking elements to reach close quarters under cover. Under such conditions, the initiative and offensive spirit of security groups using close combat weapons against tanks is of decisive importance. (See ch. 10.)

40

■ 79. WITHDRAWAL.—When the platoon executes a withdrawal, the security section covers the maneuver by fighting
a delaying action. It attempts to deceive the enemy in
regard to the movement of the platoon. Extensive use is
made of grenades, road blocks, and smoke. Maximum use
of cover and cooperation are essential in covering a withdrawal. The security section, during such action, will seldom be separated from the platoon by more than 500 yards.

■ 80. TANK HUNTING.—The security section will frequently
furnish tank hunting parties for attacks on tanks located in
parks or assembly areas. For details of tank attacking methods see chapter 10.

SECTION IV

HEAVY PLATOON

■ 81. COMPOSITION.—The tank destroyer platoon (heavy)
consists of a platoon headquarters, two tank destroyer sections, a security section, and an antiaircraft section. (See
T/O 18-27.)

■ 82. DUTIES OF PLATOON LEADER.—The platoon leader commands the platoon and is at all times responsible for its
training and discipline and the care, maintenance, and operation of its armament and equipment. On the march he
conducts the movement in compliance with the instructions
of the company commander and in conformity with the tactical situation. At halts he verifies, through reports of subordinate leaders and by personal inspection, that motor maintenance inspections are properly conducted by drivers of
all vehicles. He sees that proper march security measures
are taken. In bivouac he supervises the location of subordinate units of the platoon and verifies that the pertinent
duties indicated for personnel of the various sections are
properly performed. In combat he leads his platoon in accordance with the missions assigned by the company commander; in the absence of orders he takes such action as
will best further the mission of the company.

■ 83. TACTICAL DUTIES OF PLATOON PERSONNEL.—a. Platoon
sergeant.—The platoon sergeant is second in command. He
assists the platoon leader and replaces him when the platoon
leader is absent. The platoon leader usually marches at the

41

rear of the platoon; however, whenever the platoon leader anticipates having to leave the platoon, he causes the platoon sergeant to march with platoon headquarters. In combat he carries out-such missions as are assigned by the platoon leader. Usually, he is conveniently located with respect to the platoon leader as well as the ammunition corporal, to whom he transmits orders and signals. He assigns one observer in his vehicle to watch toward the rear.

b. Reconnaissance corporal.—The reconnaissance corporal assists the platoon leader in reconnoitering routes and positions. When not engaged in reconnaissance, he usually acts as an observer for the platoon leader. He keeps the position of the platoon and other relevant data posted on the platoon leader's map.

c. Ammunition corporal.—The ammunition corporal is in charge of the platoon ammunition vehicle. He is charged with keeping the combat vehicles constantly supplied with ammunition. This is accomplished, ordinarily, during lulls in combat. The platoon sergeant sends the ammunition vehicle to the guns requiring replenishment of ammunition. When empty, the platoon ammunition vehicle obtains replenishment of ammunition from the battalion ammunition distributing point. Movement to the battalion ammunition distributing point is effected on the order of the platoon leader; the ammunition vehicle in moving to the rear, checks in at the company command post unless the time factor is vital. The ammunition corporal at all times keeps the platoon leader informed of the amount of ammunition on hand. The platoon ammunition vehicle usually seeks cover in combat in a defiladed and concealed position in the rear of the platoon. Visual contact with the platoon sergeant or the platoon leader is maintained. Personnel on the ammunition vehicle also watch toward the rear with a view to warning the platoon of any surprise attack from that direction. Visual and other warning signals are employed.

■ 84. TACTICS.—*a. Movement.*—The platoon leader determines the march disposition of his vehicles in accordance with the situation and the orders of the company commander. Usual dispositions are as follows:

(1) When moving as a unit of the company—platoon

leader, security section, tank destroyer section, one anti-aircraft squad, tank destroyer section, second antiaircraft squad, ammunition vehicle, platoon sergeant.

(2) When the platoon is acting independently or as the advanced guard of a larger unit—security group, reinforced by one or more motorcyclists (attached from company headquarters), acting as point, followed at several hundred yards by the platoon leader, the remainder of the security section, and the rest of the platoon as previously indicated.

b. Conduct of march.—(1) The provisions of FM 25–10 as to the conduct of the march are applicable. Movement by bounds is effected when in the immediate presence of the enemy. One section of destroyers and affiliated security and antiaircraft groups may advance from cover to cover to a predetermined terrain objective while the other section overwatches the advance. The second section in turn then advances to a further objective. The platoon leader moves to successive points of observation and controls the movement by radio or visual signals.

(2) When its advance is screened, movement may be by platoon bounds. The platoon leader, with a security escort, precedes the platoon by a few hundred yards, leaving the platoon sergeant to direct the movement of the platoon. The platoon leader reaches the vicinity of the new objective in time to select suitable cover positions and direct the platoon there without halting it or delaying it in the open.

(3) The platoon in combat is usually assigned its missions in general terms. It is usually given initial positions and fire missions or the direction of advance. The platoon is not assigned a zone of action.

c. Hasty selection and occupation of position.—(1) Hasty occupation of positions will frequently be required by the situation. In such cases the platoon leader, after a hasty reconnaissance, whenever practicable assigns general areas to his section, which then take up positions with all possible speed. The platoon leader designates position areas by radio, visual signals, or provides guides.

(2) Action of this type requires instant decision by the platoon leader and immediate execution of orders by subordinate commanders. Whatever time is available between the occupation of position and the commencement of action

is utilized in improving positions. The antiaircraft and security sections are usually deployed as indicated in sections II and III of this chapter. In situations of this kind, *in the absence of orders,* individual gun commanders regulate the opening of fire and detailed adjustments of their positions on their own initiative.

d. Deliberate selection and occupation of position.—(1) The platoon leader takes part or all of the security section with him when reconnoitering a position. The security section patrols the area, covers the platoon leader's movements, and assists in reconnaissance. During the reconnaissance, the platoon usually remains under cover under control of the platoon sergeant. The latter leads it forward at a given time or upon receipt of orders or signals from the platoon leader. When kept under cover, the platoon is prepared to open fire upon short notice.

(2) Radio control by the platoon leader permits wider separation of sections than is possible between the individual destroyers of a section. A platoon, however, will seldom occupy an area larger than 500 yards square.

e. Deployment of sections.—(1) The platoon leader may deploy his tank destroyer sections in depth in vague situations, or when the flanks are exposed; however, tank destroyer sections are usually deployed abreast against a definite threat. Whenever practicable, sections are deployed so as to be mutually supporting.

(2) The platoon leader prescribes missions for the antiaircraft section and the security section when employment other than that indicated in sections II and III of this chapter is desired, and particularly when coordinated action of those units is desired in a specific area.

■ 85. COMBAT ACTION OF PLATOON.—*a.* The platoon leader in combat carries out the missions assigned him by the company commander. When no enemy tanks confront him, the platoon leader seeks and engages tanks that have passed his position or moves to the assistance of nearby platoons still engaged with the enemy, reporting such movement to his company commander.

b. During maneuvers or displacements in the presence of the enemy, the platoon usually moves by bounds, one section covering the movement of the other. When displacement is necessary, the platoon leader designates which section is to move.

c. When the platoon is held in company reserve, all destroyers are placed in firing or cover positions ready to open fire if required, but located primarily with a view to quick movement. The reserve is usually engaged by order of the company commander; in emergencies, when time is lacking to obtain instructions, the reserve commander engages the reserve on his own initiative, reporting his action as soon as practicable.

d. Following each phase of the fire fight, the platoon leader reorganizes his platoon and redistributes ammunition.

Section V

LIGHT PLATOON

■ 86. Destroyer Squad and Section.—In organization and tactical employment the subordinate units within the light platoon are generally similar to their counterparts in the heavy tank destroyer platoon.

■ 87. Light Platoon.—The light platoon is organized similarly to the heavy platoon except that it has light instead of heavy guns. Its mobility is usually greater and the destroyers, being smaller, are easier to conceal.

■ 88. Advance to Contact.—a. The light platoon is usually employed as a covering detachment (protective screen on broad front with little depth) during the advance to contact when the main body has adopted approach formation. It usually is employed to cover the advance of its own company only; it may be required to cover the advance of the battalion prior to assignment of combat missions to companies.

b. Its primary mission as covering detachment is that of security; the secondary mission is reconnaissance. It guards against surprise and obtains information by observing to the front and flanks. It pushes aside small patrols and offers resistance to larger hostile forces. It guides the force it covers over the best terrain available.

c. The covering force moves by successive bounds, the limitations of each being indicated by the commander of the covered force. Upon arriving at each terrain objective, the covering detachment halts and observes to the front and flanks until ordered to make another bound. Full advantage is taken of available cover. Upon making contact with the enemy, the platoon leader immediately informs the company commander, as the platoon will usually be preceded by its own security section, moving on a broadened front. Interval between destroyers may be as much as 200 yards.

■ 89. COMBAT.—As soon as the heavy destroyers join the action, the light platoon, in accordance with the situation and orders of the company commander, attacks the hostile covering tanks or disposes itself to protect the flanks. When protecting the flanks the platoon usually divides, one section going to the left flank, the other section to the right flank. In some instances, especially where there is strong evidence that an enemy flanking movement is developing, the company commander will withdraw the light platoon as soon as the heavy destroyers are engaged and hold it as a mobile reserve to throw against the threatened flank.

■ 90. PURSUIT.—The light platoon leads the way in pursuing a disorganized and retreating tank force. The high speed of the vehicles will be exploited to the fullest extent to intercept the enemy along his line of retreat. The platoon leader will frequently report the position of the enemy.

■ 91. SUITABILITY FOR SECURITY MISSIONS.—The light platoon is particularly suited for employment as an advance, rear, or flank guard (see FM 100–5) and to supplement security sections in protecting the remainder of the company during protracted halts or in bivouac.

■ 92. ADVANCE GUARD.—a. The platoon acting as advance guard is both a maneuvering and holding element. Its principal duties are to reconnoiter to a distance of about 800 yards to the flanks and overcome resistance encountered on the line of march or check a hostile advance until the main body can prepare for action. In case the enemy encountered is too strong for the platoon to defeat, the platoon reports the fact and reconnoiters the enemy's strength and dispositions. The platoon as advance guard is divided into an advance party and a point (see par. 74).

b. The platoon leader regulates the rate of march of the advance guard. When the movement of the main body is dependent upon information which the advance guard obtains or upon the actions of the latter, the advance guard regulates the rate of march. At night it is usual for the advance guard to regulate the march.

c. The main body usually follows the advance guard at 3 to 5 minutes' interval.

d. When moving by bounds, the platoon coordinates its advance with the rear vehicle of the point, so far as practicable. When contact is gained, the leading vehicles of the point remain near the axis of march and engage the enemy by fire. The platoon leader makes a hasty reconnaissance and determines his course of action. Usually he extends reconnaissance to locate the flanks, drive out the enemy, or develop the situation. If the resistance is too strong to be overcome, the platoon is disposed to cover the approach of the main body.

e. A platoon acting as advance guard will usually be required to act as covering detachment for the battalion when the latter begins the approach march.

■ 93. FLANK GUARD.—a. When a suitable route is available, the flank guard usually marches parallel to the main body. A reconnoitering patrol is pushed well forward; the bulk of the flank guard usually moves abreast of leading elements of the main body, halting at sensitive points as required by the situation. When several such locations must be passed during the progress of a march, the flank guard moves by bounds from one position to another. Upon arrival at a locality, dispositions are made to hold that position as long as may be necessary to allow the main body to march out of danger. The flank guard then moves rapidly to the next locality.

b. When the locality from which an attack may be expected is well defined, the platoon may deploy to defend a key position until the command has passed.

c. Where considerable doubt exists as to the avenue of hostile approach, the platoon may be held in a position of readiness at some conveniently located point.

d. When the enemy is encountered, the flank guard may act offensively, delay in successive positions, or defend a position, in accordance with instructions and the situation.

■ 94. REAR GUARD.—*a.* When the distance from the enemy permits, a platoon acting as rear guard moves in march formation. It drops back a rear point which adheres closely to the route of march, observing constantly to the flanks and rear. It discourages pursuit by firing on hostile elements.

b. When in contact with the enemy, the rear guard moves on a broad front and opens fire at long range to force the enemy to deploy and thus delay his advance. Unless the security of the main body requires a stubborn resistance, the rear guard avoids close range combat and withdraws successively from position to position as the enemy approaches. When necessary it maneuvers at distances up to about 800 yards on either side of the axis of movement.

c. The rear guard fights in successive positions. A rear guard position should favor withdrawal by affording covered routes of withdrawal. The rear guard commander makes timely provision for preliminary reconnaissance of new positions and routes thereto.

d. When the enemy presses his pursuit closely, greater resistance is offered. Full use is made of surprise attacks and ambushes to slow down or halt the hostile advance.

e. A rear guard resorts to such defensive measures for halt- ing or delaying the enemy as obstructing fords, executing demolitions within the capabilities of the rear guard, felling trees across the road, burning stretches of grass or shrubs, or by the use of mines and persistent chemicals.

SECTION VI

TANK DESTROYER COMPANY

■ 95. COMPOSITION.—The tank destroyer company comprises a company headquarters, one light platoon, and two heavy platoons.

■ 96. EQUIPMENT AND TRANSPORTATION.—For authorized equipment and transportation, see T/O 18–27. A baggage truck and a kitchen truck with trailer are furnished by the transportation platoon of headquarters company.

■ 97. COMMUNICATION.—The company commander has a two-way radio equipped with two receivers; one receiver is in the company net, the other in the battalion net.

■ 98. COMPANY COMMANDER.—The company commander commands the company and is responsible for its training and discipline.

■ 99. COMPANY EXECUTIVE.—The company executive is the second in command; he assists the company commander and acts for him in his absence. The executive is charged with organization and security of the command post, including the maintenance and supply group (when present) and motorcyclists. He maintains communication with battalion headquarters and keeps that organization constantly informed. The executive officer at times will act in the capacity of a reconnaissance officer. In this event his regular duties as executive officer will be taken over by the first sergeant. As reconnaissance officer he assists the company commander in the reconnaissance of routes, assembly, and attack positions.

■ 100. OTHER COMPANY PERSONNEL.—*a. First sergeant.*—The first sergeant supervises the establishment and operation of the command post. He assists the supply and maintenance groups and keeps the operations map, journal, and message files. He takes over the duties of the executive officer when the latter is performing reconnaissance missions.

b. Signal sergeant.—The signal sergeant is responsible for establishing and maintaining radio communication; he operates the company net control station; he rides in the company commander's vehicle.

c. Motor sergeant.—The motor sergeant is responsible for the proper maintenance of all organizational transportation. During combat the motor sergeant joins company headquarters. He is charged with the recovery and prompt repair of all vehicles. He utilizes such equipment as may be put at his disposal by the company commander. During combat he and the mechanics repair disabled combat vehicles which have been towed to covered or defiladed positions during lulls in the action.

49

d. Reconnaissance corporal.—The reconnaissance corporal assists in the reconnaissance of positions and routes; he acts as an observer; he guides platoons to positions.

e. Bugler.—The bugler serves as a guide, messenger, and observer. He also serves, along with chauffeurs, as a rifleman in the local defense of the command post.

f. Messengers.—In addition to the reconnaissance corporal, there are mounted messengers (motorcycles and a ¼-ton truck). They are used for column control and route marking. When the use of radio is not feasible, they are employed as messengers. In combat they are engaged on scouting or observing missions.

g. Motorcyclists.—Duties of motorcyclists when acting as scouts are covered in the chapter on the reconnaissance company.

■ 101. OCCUPATION OF BIVOUAC.—*a.* In a battalion bivouac the destroyer company generally will be assigned a sector for local security. It will maintain contact with adjacent units. Positions will be selected to take advantage of natural concealment and to permit local defense against air attack (dispersion and cover) and ground attack (maneuver room, routes, and natural obstacles).

b. If there is good concealment offered by trees or brush, the interval between vehicles may be reduced to 25 yards; if concealment is scanty the minimum interval is 50 yards. Where there is no concealment the vehicles will be widely scattered (at least 100 yards) and every effort made to take advantage of irregularities of the ground to minimize damage from bomb or shell fragments. Small vehicles such as ¼-ton trucks and motorcycles may be grouped in pairs. Slit trenches will be dug by all personnel; this is especially important for those whose vehicles carry no armor. (See **FM** 31–25.)

c. Security squads reinforced by 37-mm guns will be posted to cover avenues of approach into the company position and to protect company headquarters. Except when the terrain offers slight choice, weapons posted to cover roads should not be in the immediate vicinity of the road itself. The company commander coordinates disposition of the various antiaircraft sections.

d. Habitually, all motor vehicles are parked in bivouac so that they can move out without backing or turning. All vehicles face outward or toward the nearest route of egress.

■ 102. MOVEMENT.—*a.* The usual order of march for a tank destroyer company forming part of the main body of a battalion is company command echelon, the light platoon, the heavy platoons. When the company constitutes the advance guard of a battalion, the order of march may be the light platoon (advance party), portions of the battalion command echelon, company command echelon, and the heavy platoons as the support. The antiaircraft section of the leading heavy platoon will frequently be detailed to furnish protection for the battalion command post, one gun moving at the head and one at rear of the command post. The motor sergeant and one or two mechanics mounted on a ¼-ton truck will bring up the rear of the column. All other maintenance and supply elements usually will remain in the battalion rear echelon.

b. March dispositions and route security are prescribed by the company commander. For concealment, movement will often be by bounds, and occasionally, by infiltration. In areas providing no concealment (flat, treeless plains, deserts, etc.) wide intervals between vehicles will be maintained.

c. When elements of the reconnaissance company are attached to tank destroyer companies, reconnaissance missions are assigned them as follows:

(1) To secure information of hostile tank forces, their size, disposition, composition, and direction of movement.

(2) To assist in leading tank destroyer companies to assembly positions or initial combat locations.

(3) To provide a local warning service.
Tank destroyer companies will employ their motorcyclists for close reconnaissance, security, and liaison missions, usually in collaboration with the light platoon.

d. On moving into the combat zone, the company will be on the alert with guns prepared for action. Information of the enemy and friendly situation will be passed down *through all ranks.* A company rallying position is designated, usually one or two miles in rear of the area of expected combat.

e. Before moving forward to engage hostile forces, the gun vehicles and the platoon ammunition carriers will enter combat with the maximum of ammunition. Resupply of fuel will be effected. If trucks carrying ammunition and fuel have been attached to the tank destroyer companies upon their entrance into the combat zone, these follow the rear elements of the tank destroyer companies.

■ 103. RECONNAISSANCE OF POSITIONS.—Prior to the arrival of: the company, the company commander reconnoiters the area in which his unit is to be deployed, to the extent permitted by the situation. He effects this reconnaissance in person when the situation permits; in other cases, he may detail an officer for this task. The company commander is accompanied by a small party, which secures the movement and assists in the reconnaissance. When time is pressing, the company commander's reconnaissance will be restricted to a hasty observation of the area from the best available point of vantage, as a result of which he assigns areas for his platoons. He usually employs the light platoon to cover the occupation of positions by the heavy platoons.

■ 104. IMMEDIATE ACTION MANEUVERS.—*a.* The following maneuvers will make it possible for immediate action to be taken by a company when an enemy is met unexpectedly:

(1) *Protective maneuver.*—On the order: FIRST (SECOND,. THIRD) PLATOON, PROTECTION FRONT, the subordinate unit referred to moves out ahead of the main unit and forms a protective screen. The distance the subordinate unit moves out depends on the local situation. The order PROTECTION FRONT may be varied to PROTECTION RIGHT (LEFT, REAR) as the situation demands. The platoon in such case is deployed by approved commands or signals.

(2) *Attack maneuver.*—The first subordinate unit to meet the enemy halts in the nearest favorable position and engages the enemy with fire, while the remainder of the unit maneuvers to attack the enemy. The attack will be along a flank or along some covered line of approach, if one exists. Every effort will be made to deliver fire from positions of at least partial hull defilade. This maneuver is based on the following orders which are given over the radio or by visual signal. The unit or units to execute the maneuver are designated in the order—

ENVELOP RIGHT FLANK.
ENVELOP LEFT FLANK.
DOUBLE ENVELOPMENT.

b. The company commander moves under cover of the tank destroyer unit which is engaging the enemy by fire to a position from which he can best see the combat area, and issues such further orders as are necessary.

c. These maneuvers are intended for use when opposition is met unexpectedly. They are not the best methods to meet every situation and whenever possible more detailed orders should be issued.

d. When a tank destroyer unit has thoroughly mastered the execution of these maneuvers, they may be designated by numbers or other simple code designation.

e. Platoon leaders should be cautioned that energy and initiative must be used in the application of immediate action maneuvers; their successful use depends upon the adaptation of the movement to the particular situation.

■ 105. COMBAT.—*a.* If the enemy has been located, the company may establish an ambush or plan a surprise attack upon the enemy when he is not prepared to maneuver. Either operation requires thorough reconnaissance and concealed movement to combat positions. In vague situations the company will be preceded by the light platoon and at times by elements of the reconnaissance company. The light platoon will be employed in forward areas, the heavy platoons being employed when the direction of hostile armored attack becomes known. When the heavy platoons are in position, the lighter guns may then be brought back and used to cover the flanks or take post in reserve.

b. In deploying for action, care is taken lest an excellent field of fire result in the concentration of an excessive number of guns to cover a limited area, thus decreasing the ability of a unit to meet a tank attack from flank or rear.

c. When the direction of the hostile advance is known, and particularly when there is opportunity for ambush, part or all of the heavier guns are engaged at the outset. In such case the company retains a reserve of some guns, light or heavy.

d. Initial deployment against a tank attack should provide a checkerboarded arrangement of weapons affording one another mutual support by flanking fire in a manner generally similar to machine-gun dispositions.

e. Reserves are usually held under cover near routes facilitating movement in any direction. Wide dispersion will be avoided, except for concealment and protection; anticipated firing positions near the reserves and routes thereto are reconnoitered and, in case of emergency, occupied.

f. (1) While the fire fight is in progress, the company commander, so far as practicable, leaves control of detailed movement to platoon leaders. Except for the transmission of essential data and orders he endeavors to leave the radio net clear for them.

(2) During initial phases the company commander plans the further employment of his unit; this is dependent upon the result of early encounters and the reactions of the hostile tanks. The company commander keeps in close touch with the progress of the combat by personal observation, moving from one platoon combat area to another, and by listening to radio reports.

(3) Depending upon the situation, he shifts combat platoons to counter the movement of tanks around the flanks of the destroyers, engages the reserve platoon, or moves the entire company to a better area from which to attack.

(4) He causes necessary route reconnaissance to be conducted in anticipation of movements to new combat areas. During lulls, he causes ammunition to be redistributed among platoons when such action is necessary.

■ **106. PURSUIT.**—*a.* When the company constitutes the encircling force, the company commander seeks to delay the enemy by attacks against the flanks or head of his column with the light platoon, to facilitate placing the heavy platoons in advantageous positions across his route of retreat.

b. When the company is detailed to exert direct pressure on the retreating enemy, it moves boldly on as broad a front as the road net and terrain permit. In open terrain when in close contact with the enemy, all platoons are engaged. When the terrain restricts rapid movement to a single route, the light platoon leads.

■ 107. REORGANIZATION.—*a.* The order to break off contact with the enemy will be given by the company commander, and a new rallying position designated if the company has moved a great distance during the course of the combat.

b. When control is regained through reassembly at the rallying position, new orders will be issued. Such reorganization and regrouping may be an intermediate bound in a movement toward a battalion rallying position or may be a preliminary step toward a new offensive maneuver.

■ 108. ATTACHED CHEMICAL TROOPS.—*a.* In the absence of organic 81-mm mortars, a chemical mortar and crew or, in exceptional cases, a chemical platoon may be attached to the company. In the latter case the mortars are usually distributed to tank destroyer platoons unless specific need for massed employment of the chemical platoon can be foreseen.

b. On the march the mortar vehicle usually moves with company headquarters.

c. In combat the mortar remains near the company commander initially, prepared to move to any part of the company area to execute such missions as may be assigned. The mortar vehicle is vulnerable to fire of all types and its crew is not afforded armor protection; it must be kept in defiladed positions, so far as practicable. Single missions are assigned successively, each specific task being executed on order.

d. Missions usually assigned are—

(1) To place smoke on hostile assault guns and tanks which are covering by fire the advance of maneuvering tanks.

(2) To screen displacements and withdrawals of tank destroyers by the use of smoke.

e. When attached to a platoon, the mortar operates directly under the platoon leader.

CHAPTER 5

RECONNAISSANCE COMPANY

Section I

SCOUTS

■ 109. General.—The success of reconnaissance elements and of tank destroyer combat in general frequently depends upon the ability, intelligence, and aggressiveness of the scout. Therefore, the scout is carefully selected and rigidly trained for the duty required of him. Mounted scouting is performed on motorcycles and other light vehicles; however, every scout is thoroughly grounded in dismounted patrolling (see FM 21-45) and in the methods of tank hunting described in chapter 10.

■ 110. Mission.—The primary mission of the scout is to obtain information of the enemy and relay it to the next reconnaissance echelon in time for it to be of maximum value. He may be required to determine whether the enemy occupies a particular area or is using a specific route; the enemy's strength, location, composition, and movement; the status of roads, culverts, bridges, or other construction; the extent and nature of defiles, etc. Observation alone seldom reveals information of a well-concealed enemy. Mounted or dismounted, as necessary, the scout approaches suspected enemy localities, forcing the enemy to disclose his presence. Scouts preferably operate in pairs or groups, although on occasion they may operate to best advantage individually.

■ 111. Movement by Day.—In order to observe the enemy and not be seen, a scout must conceal his movements. A thorough knowledge of camouflage and terrain appreciation is essential. In exposed areas the scout moves rapidly from cover to cover and remains motionless in observation, searching the area to his front, after which he continues to advance. In enemy territory he moves by bounds, either mounted or dismounted. In close country bounds are short; in open country they are longer. To avoid detection the scout should cut the motor and coast his vehicle whenever possible. Because of the characteristics of his vehicle, the scout resorts frequently to dismounted action. He is constantly concerned with the necessity for concealing his vehicle during pauses, for observation and work on foot; he places it so as to facilitate reversal of direction or change of route if necessary. A mounted scout can move long distances on roads by day or night, and when the terrain is favorable he can make progress across country. The speed with which he can move compensates to some extent for the fact that a mounted scout is more likely to attract attention than a man on foot. If attacked suddenly, the scout takes up a hasty firing position and returns the fire, or immediately moves to cover if it is available. (See FM 21–45.)

■ 112. MOVEMENT BY NIGHT.—At night the scout usually operates without lights, and if practicable remains on or adjacent to the axis of advance (roads and trails). The noise of the motor is audible for considerable distances on a silent night, and it is difficult for the scout to see or hear much while in motion. He progresses by bounds from one terrain feature to another, stops at the end of each bound, if necessary, and proceeds on foot to look and listen for the information he seeks. The scout should know exactly what he is expected to do. He should study his map and the terrain he must traverse and plan his procedure accordingly. His orders are usually given to him orally, and he is permitted to record only such data as will be of no value to the enemy. Orders to scouts are similar to orders given patrol leaders. (See par. 132e.)

■ 113. GUIDING UNITS.—Each column is guided by competent scouts who employ their knowledge of distances, map reading, stars, and landmarks to guide their units correctly. When feasible, scouts should go over the route by day, making mental and written notes of key points and landmarks. At each critical point, such as a road junction, or when the route changes direction, the scout remains until

57

relieved or until the last unit passes that point. Whenever a column subdivides or leaves a road to go into assembly positions prior to action, it is essential that well-informed scouts help guide the units. Scouts from tank destroyer companies may be attached to the reconnaissance company for this purpose. For navigation under desert conditions, see FM 31-25.

SECTION II

RECONNAISSANCE SECTION AND PLATOON

■ 114. RECONNAISSANCE SECTION.—The reconnaissance section is equipped with an armored reconnaissance car; several lighter vehicles (¼ ton), and at least one motorcycle. Sections preferably operate as a unit. A section constitutes a suitable reconnaissance patrol.

■ 115. PATROL MISSIONS.—*a*. Reconnaissance missions require the section to obtain information of the enemy or of the terrain. Reconnaissance patrols regulate their actions with respect to the enemy and avoid combat, except for self-protection, or when *accomplishment of the mission* requires combat.

b. Security missions require the section to protect other units from surprise or interference by the enemy. A security patrol regulates its action on the unit to be protected and frequently must engage in combat.

c. The number and strength of patrols should be the minimum required by the situation. As far as practicable, the integrity of sections and platoons should be preserved. Officers lead important patrols. Patrols are given specific missions.

■ 116. PREPARATION FOR PATROL DUTY.—*a*. After receiving his mission (see par. 132) and making necessary preliminary arrangements, the patrol leader issues his orders, covering the items listed below. When time permits, a warning order will be issued incorporating all information then available.

(1) Information of the enemy and friendly troops.

(2) Mission of the patrol and plan of the patrol leader for accomplishing the mission, including objectives, route, and initial information desired.

(3) Designation of men and vehicles for flank reconnais-

sance and other duties; designation of first assembly point (and alternate), and orders regarding general conduct, including combat.

(4) Instruction as to carrying of additional type C rations, water, oil, and fuel.

(5) The points to which messages should be sent and the designation of a second in command. Whether or not the patrol will engage in combat, if it can be avoided.

b. The patrol leader satisfies himself that all members understand their orders and their individual assignments. The leader and the second in command should know the location of the reconnaissance company command post and its route.

c. Patrol leaders should have wire cutters, watch, compass, message blanks, pencil, flashlight, field glasses, and maps; codes and other documents of value to the enemy will not be carried. The patrol should carry rations (including water) for the duration of the mission. The patrol starts, whenever practicable, with extra oil and fuel containers.

■ 117. CONDUCT OF PATROL.—a. The conduct of a reconnaissance patrol varies with the mission, situation, terrain, and estimated distance from the enemy.

b. When a large area must be rapidly reconnoitered or when there is no indication of the presence of hostile elements, reconnaissance patrols move rapidly in open formation along the route, halting to observe only at critical points or if suspicious activity is noted.

c. In the presence of the enemy, the patrol usually moves by bounds, halting briefly on successive objectives such as the more important terrain features. Between objectives the patrol advances by successive echelons from one observation point to another. While one echelon covers the advance, the other goes ahead of the next crest or objective and stops under cover while scouts dismount and reconnoiter. Upon signal that all is clear, the second echelon advances to the first. Between observation points movement is rapid. A third echelon may be held in reserve. It follows the other cautiously, brings back information in case the leading elements are ambushed, and pays particular attention to routes leading from the flanks. The armored reconnaissance vehicle usually is employed to cover the movements of the advanced echelon. When minor resistance is encountered, part of the first echelon executes an outflanking maneuver or "side-slip." When necessary, other echelons move farther to a flank to reduce the resistance or ascertain its extent. Unless the accomplishment of the mission demands combat, the entire patrol may side-slip such resistance, reporting by radio or messenger to rear units of the reconnaissance company information of the resistance located and the action of the patrol. If an attack is made, the reconnaissance patrol avoids becoming so closely engaged as to lose its freedom of maneuver.

d. Cross-country patrols may move in diamond, wedge, or column formation, depending on the situation and terrain. When deployed in the presence of the enemy, the ¼-ton trucks usually take the leading and flank positions. The armored vehicle covers them from the rear. The motor-cyclist acts as getaway man and messenger. So far as practicable, it moves along roads and trails. When the advanced echelon or point is fired upon, vehicles usully move to the nearest cover.

e. For reconnaissance of important objectives dismounted scouts with portable radios may be directed to vantage points whence they relay information to the section.

f. When passing through a village, over a bridge, or through a defile, in the presence of the enemy, scouts are covered by the remainder of the patrol from a position on the near side with guns sighted on possible hostile positions. If covering fire is not considered necessary, the rear elements follow the leading element at supporting distance. Whenever practicable, the patrol bypasses obstacles and reconnoiters them from the rear.

g. Patrols reconnoitering a hostile column on the march can best perform this mission by observation from several successive positions on the flank of the column. Reconnaissance of an enemy bivouac or tank park requires dismounted scouts or patrols to investigate the locality from several directions.

h. The location of a suspected ambush is reconnoitered by observing from a vantage point. If no road block is visible and time is pressing, scouts rush forward prepared to open fire, while remaining vehicles halt and are prepared to cover the scouts by supporting fire. If time permits, it is best for the scouts to reconnoiter the suspected area on foot. A located ambush is avoided unless the mission or situation requires its reduction. If the ambush must be reduced, it is attacked from front and flank. To extricate a vehicle caught in ambush, remaining vehicles of the patrol maneuver to give it fire support, but do not close in to the ambush.

i. A reconnaissance section employed as a mobile security detachment on the front, flanks, or rear of a tank destroyer unit gives prompt warning to the unit protected of the approach or location of hostile forces, and opposes the latter in the degree required by its mission and the situation.

j. Unless so ordered, a patrol does not stop for a prolonged rest before returning. If necessary to remain out overnight or to make a prolonged halt, the patrol avoids villages, farms, and inclosures in selecting a bivouac. The position chosen should provide concealment from both ground and air observation and several routes of movement therefrom. It should offer opportunities for observation, defense, and departure. In daytime it should be near high ground offering distant all-around observation. At night it should be on low ground so as to bring approaching persons into view against the sky. By night or day, front, flanks, and rear are protected by observation.

k. At all times, patrols will be on the alert to discover areas that have been contaminated with persistent gases. Reports of such areas and safe routes through or around them will be forwarded promptly to the company commander. (See TF 7–275 and 7–280.)

■ 118. COMBAT MISSIONS.—*a.* The section leader determines when combat is necessary for the success of reconnaissance or security missions. He keeps in mind the consideration that the best reconnaisance is generally performed by stealth.

b. When deployed for combat in conjunction with other elements, ¼-ton trucks are usually disposed to the front and flanks of the armored vehicle. The motorcyclist is employed as directed for messenger service, reconnaissance, and observation. The combat action of the section conforms, generally, to the conduct indicated for the light destroyer squad and security section.

■ 119. COUNTERRECONNAISSANCE PATROLS.—*a.* The section act-. ing as a counterreconnaissance patrol locates and destroys hostile patrols and warns counterreconnaissance detachments of the presence and movement of larger hostile elements that are beyond the capability of the patrol to destroy. They delay such forces.

b. In a moving screen, patrols move along routes which enable them to keep under observation the likely routes of hostile advance. They patrol laterally to adjacent patrols.

c. In stationary screens, patrols are posted at observation points from which they can view routes of hostile approach. Active patrolling between adjoining groups is maintained.

■ 120. RECONNAISSANCE PLATOON.—The reconnaissance platoon consists of two sections. The platoon leader employs them as a platoon or by section to execute the missions assigned him.

■ 121. RECONNAISSANCE MISSIONS.—When the zone assigned for reconnaissance is wide or contains more than one axial road, the platoon leader may divide the zone between his sections. When the platoon is assigned to reconnoiter a narrow zone or single road, sections usually move by successive bounds. Elements of the rear or supporting section may be dispatched to reconnoiter flanks or critical points. The same section is always in front, halting or slowing at intervals to observe and allow the supporting section to catch up, then moving out again. The platoon leader is usually at the head of the supporting section.

■ 122. SECURITY MISSIONS.—The performance of reconnaissance missions by reconnaissance platoons is in itself a security measure. In addition the platoon may be assigned security missions. It is well fitted for employment as a mobile security detachment on the front, flanks, or rear of a battalion. It may operate under the control of the company commander or be attached to other units. Security missions are executed as indicated for destroyer company units.

■ 123. COMBAT.—*a. When engaged.*—A reconnaissance platoon engages in combat when necessary to accomplish its mission or when necessary for self-preservation.

b. Initial contact.—(1) When the enemy is sighted before

he sees the platoon, every precaution is taken to prevent disclosing the platoon's presence. The leading vehicle on observing the enemy halts at the nearest cover and informs the platoon leader, who transmits the information to the other elements of the platoon and immediately makes a personal reconnaissance. The rear elements keep the platoon leader under observation for signals and place their vehicles so as to cover the flanks and rear of the platoon. If the mission and immediate situation require combat, the platoon leader decides whether to employ offensive or defensive action. When combat is incidental to securing identifications or engaging hostile reconnaissance vehicles, an ambush is set. Consideration must always be given to the terrain, road net, and mutual supporting action between elements of the platoon.

(2) When the leading vehicle is taken under surprise fire, or surprises a hostile force, it utilizes its maximum fire power to inflict the greatest possible damage at once, and quickly seeks cover from which to continue its fire fight. The platoon commander, informed of the encounter by personal observation, the sound of firing, or by message, must decide promptly whether to attack, defend, or evade. When the mission permits, offensive action by fire and movement against one of the enemy's flanks often affords the best chance of success. Regardless of how the leader plans to handle the situation, he should provide assistance, at once, for the leading car by taking his own car or sending another to a position where supporting fire can be delivered on the enemy. If the hostile force consists of mechanized vehicles, at least one tank destroyer gun should be placed in action immediately. His next immediate concern is to assure himself that his platoon is so disposed that his flanks and rear are reasonably secure. If he has run into a force stronger than his own, he promptly breaks off the action unless this is contrary to his mission. If in doubt, he may maintain contact and dispose his platoon for defense while making further investigation. Even though his platoon is well disposed for its own security, and appears to have the initial advantage, he does not commit it to an attack unless his mission justifies an attack and a personal reconnaissance convinces him that an attack will succeed.

c. Attack of road blocks.—(1) When the platoon encounters a road block, dismounted reconnaissance is made to determine the nature and extent of the obstacle; whether it is isolated or merely one of a series; whether it is defended, and, if so, in what strength and by what type of weapons; and whether if can be detoured. If a detour is practicable, the platoon detours the road block and continues on its mission, reporting promptly, and in detail, the information obtained. When detour is impracticable or reconnaissance reveals a weak defense, the platoon may attack.

(2) The method of attack of a road block will depend on the location, strength, and composition of the hostile defending troops. Usually part of the platoon is employed near the axis of movement to engage the enemy by fire, while the remainder, utilizing surprise to the maximum, maneuvers to a favorable position on the flank or in the rear and attacks by fire and movement. Stalking is particularly applicable in such action.

d. Delaying action.—(1) When the platoon is employed to seize and hold distant objectives, its combat action frequently takes the form of delaying action in advance of the assigned objective. If a strong defensive position is available, such as a defile, vehicles are dispersed under cover in good firing position and a portion of the platoon prepares for dismounted action.

(2) In delaying action the platoon occupies successive positions between the hostile force and its objective, forcing the enemy to deploy frequently for attack. One section usually goes into action in an advanced position, opening fire at long ranges while the other occupies a position in rear to cover its withdrawal or executes a surprise attack against the enemy's flank. Ambushes are prepared in favorable localities. Withdrawing individual vehicles withdraw successively, mutually supporting one another.

e. Harassing action.—In harassing action the platoon annoys and wears down the hostile resistance by surprise attacks against the enemy's front, flanks, and rear and by ambush operations.

■ 124. COUNTERRECONNAISSANCE.—*a.* The missions of a platoon acting as a counterreconnaissance detachment are, primarily, to prevent reconnaissance by the enemy's ground troops and

64

to deny the transmission of information to the enemy. The platoon is habitually assigned a zone of action or a sector. For general doctrine governing counterreconnaissance, see FM 100-5.

b. The width of the zone of action or the frontage assigned depends upon the strength of the hostile forces likely to be encountered, the terrain and road net, and the nature of the screen to be established. A platoon will not usually be assigned a frontage wider than 3 miles.

c. In general, counterreconnaissance detachments will often be used to—

(1) Prevent small hostile patrols from penetrating the zone of action or sector assigned.

(2) Destroy or drive off small hostile detachments.

(3) Locate and delay the advance of larger detachments.

(4) Reinforce, or form rallying positions for, their own patrols.

(5) Maintain liaison within that part of the screen established by the detachment as well as with adjacent detachments.

(6) Reconnoiter locally to the front and flanks of the detachment.

(7) Furnish information to the commander of the main body.

d. Personnel and weapons are employed in accordance with the doctrine of their use in offensive and defensive action by small units.

SECTION III

PIONEER PLATOON

■ **125. ORGANIZATION.**—For composition, armament, and equipment, see T/O 18-28.

■ **126. CHARACTERISTICS AND MISSIONS.**—*a.* The pioneer platoon is organized, equipped, and especially trained for the performance of combat engineer tasks. Its armament is relatively limited, but the platoon is capable of protecting itself for a limited time against attack by dismounted enemy elements.

b. The principal missions of the platoon are—

(1) To facilitate the movement of the battalion or elements thereof.

(2) To impede the movement of enemy vehicles by obstacles and demolitions.

c. Other employment of the platoon may be for security, battle reconnaissance, route marking, or as a reserve of dismounted troops.

d. The pioneer platoon is usually employed under the direction of the reconnaissance company commander. When its mission requires it to be detached so far that it is removed from the immediate control of the company commander, it may operate directly under the battalion commander.

■ 127. TACTICAL EMPLOYMENT.—a. In a bivouac or assembly position, the platoon helps to provide the static antimechanized measures, mines, road blocks, etc., necessary to secure the area from hostile attack.

b. During the march of the battalion, unless otherwise ordered, the pioneer platoon marches with the reconnaissance company, on the main axis of advance. The platoon commander's radio is kept tuned to the frequency of the company commander's transmitter. Where removal of obstacles is necessary to permit the advance, the platoon moves rapidly to the designated area and performs its tasks. The platoon may be required to protect the flank of the battalion by the establishment of hasty road blocks or execution of demolition on routes of enemy approach. During the march the platoon leader also carefully notes all defiles, bridges, and areas suitable for demolition or obstacle construction in case such action should become necessary owing to an altered situation.

c. Immediately prior to combat the pioneer platoon may be employed to improve routes into proposed areas of employment. During the actual movement into combat, the pioneer platoon, or detachments thereof, may march with forward elements of tank destroyer companies to assist their movement.

d. If an ambush engagement is planned, this platoon may be used to reinforce the unit posted to delay the head of the hostile armored elements by use of road blocks or mines.

e. After the action the pioneer platoon may be used to prepare the rallying position and assist in securing it.

f. Should the action develop so favorably as to cause the

battalion commander to initiate pursuit, the pioneer platoon is used with the reconnaissance company in an encircling action, to block defiles and execute demolitions on the enemy's line of retreat.

g. If the battalion withdraws, the demolition capabilities of the pioneer platoon are employed to the fullest in hindering the pursuit.

■ 128. USE OF MINES.—Placing of mines by the pioneer platoon is a temporary measure; except when precluded by the situation, the mines are recovered by the platoon before it leaves the vicinity. Prompt report is made to the battalion commander concerning the location of mines. The platoon posts the necessary guards and takes the other precautions necessary to prevent mines from damaging friendly vehicles.

SECTION IV

RECONNAISSANCE COMPANY

■ 129. GENERAL.—*a.* The reconnaissance company consists of a company headquarters, a pioneer platoon, and three reconnaissance platoons.

b. It is the principal reconnaissance agency of the tank destroyer battalion. Its mobility on roads or cross country and its fire power make it capable of both offensive and defensive action during either reconnaissance or security operations.

c. Whenever practicable, the reconnaissance company maintains a radio set in the air-ground net.

d. The assignment of missions and the issuance of reconnaissance instructions will be greatly expedited by standing operating procedure, especially with reference to information which is habitually desired. For example, suitable items which may be obtained coincident with the performance of other missions and pertinent information thereof transmitted at designated times or places are—

(1) Routes and bridges, their type and construction.

(2) Communication facilities and other utilities.

(3) Location of contaminated areas.

(4) Location and type of supplies, especially gasoline, oil, and food.

(5) Location and time of all hostile contact.

(6) Type, location, and direction of flight of hostile aircraft.

(7) Type, location, and movement of hostile mechanized elements.

(8) Other pertinent information as to terrain.

■ 130. MISSIONS.—*a.* (1) The principal mission of the company will usually be to obtain information of the enemy, friendly troops, and the terrain and to transmit such information to the battalion commander in time for it to be acted upon. Other missions which may be assigned are to provide security for the battalion, to guide it on the march, to facilitate its movement through pioneer action, and, exceptionally, to participate in combat. Assignment of all of these missions for simultaneous execution will be unusual.

(2) The company at all times has a concurrent mission of discovering areas contaminated by persistent gases and safe passages or detours when these areas are along a route to be used by the battalion or elements thereof.

b. At times it will be necessary for the company to perform both reconnaissance and security missions simultaneously. When both types of missions are given, the battalion commander should indicate whether reconnaissance or security is of the greater importance. The reconnaissance company commander with this in mind allots the missions to subordinate elements of his company, assigning stronger forces to the more important mission. Under no circumstances should a subordinate element, such as a platoon, be given both reconnaissance and security missions simultaneously. It may be necessary, however, as the situation changes, to assign a reconnaissance mission to an element which had previously been assigned a security mission or vice versa. When such an occasion arises, it must be made clear to the element that its assignment to the original mission is terminated.

c. In allotting missions, the company commander endeavors to retain at least one reconnaissance platoon in reserve.

■ 131. OCCUPATION OF BIVOUAC.—*a.* The reconnaissance company bivouacs with the remainder of the battalion; usually it is located near the principal route of egress from the bivouac. It posts local security in a manner similar to that indicated for tank destroyer companies. In exposed situations, elements of the reconnaissance company provide stationary observation posts along main routes several miles from the bivouac.

b. When near the enemy the bulk of the company will often be employed on reconnaissance and security missions away from the bivouac. During hours of darkness, reconnaissance elements not in contact with the enemy or observing important avenues of tank approach will be habitually withdrawn to the bivouac area of the battalion unless an emergency calls for other action.

■ 132. RECONNAISSANCE.—*a.* A reconnaissance company under average conditions can reconnoiter a zone from 10 to 20 miles wide containing from three to five axial roads generally parallel to the direction of advance at the rate of 8 to 15 miles an hour.

b. The battalion commander's instructions to the reconnaissance company commander for the execution of reconnaissance will usually include—

(1) Information concerning the enemy.

(2) Information of friendly troops, and the axis of advance of the battalion command post.

(3) Mission of the batallion.

(4) Areas or zones to be reconnoitered and information needed.

(5) Time and place at which information is desired and means of transmission (radio or messenger).

c. The company commander's orders to platoon and detached patrol leaders are usually oral; special reconnaissance instructions may be written.

d. Warning orders are issued when time permits. These include information as to—

Mission.
Time of starting.
Reinforcements, if any.
Gasoline, oil, ammunition, equipment, and rations.
Maps.

e. Following the warning order, detailed instructions are issued. They contain general and special instructions.

(1) General instructions include—

(a) Information of the enemy which has a direct bearing on the mission.

(b) Mission, time of departure, route, and objectives of the main body.

(c) Information of other reconnaissance or security agencies, particularly adjacent reconnaissance units.

(d) Mission, route, and objectives of the company.

(2) Special instructions include—

(a) Special information required (stated in the form of a specific question or assigned as a specific mission).

(b) Zone, area, or route to be covered.

(c) Objectives and time each is to be reached.

(d) Reconnaissance phase lines and time each is to be crossed.

(e) Instructions for transmission of reports or time when reports are desired.

(f) Line of conduct to be pursued in the presence of the enemy or in case hostile patrols are encountered.

(g) Instructions concerning communication with observation aviation.

(h) When and where platoon or patrol must rejoin.

(i) Location of company command post.

f. The company commander divides the zone to be reconnoitered among his reconnaissance platoons in accordance with its width and the number of axial roads. In principle, he assigns one road to a platoon. He rarely makes a platoon responsible for reconnoitering a zone wider than 5 miles.

g. The use of radio is limited, usually, to the transmission of important information immediately to the battalion commander. Overlays and sketches are often utilized to assist the battalion commander in visualizing the terrain and to facilitate rapid planning.

■ 133. RECONNAISSANCE IN FORCE.—a. During the early phases of an operation, the location, and at times the composition and strength, of leading hostile elements may be determined by observation and light contact, but as the main forces of the enemy approach, this may be insufficient. To determine the location, strength, and movement of the main body of enemy tanks may require reconnaissance in force.

b. The reconnaissance company commander determines,

upon available information, whether he should make a reconnaissance in force and where he should direct it. When practicable, he reports the situation and his contemplated action to the battalion commander.

c. If the reconnaissance in force encounters superior forces, the company breaks off the attack. If the company also has been assigned a security mission, it maintains contact, fighting a delaying action where necessary.

d. If contact with the main hostile force is developed by this action, the company informs the battalion and remains in observation; if the opposition proves to be merely local security or reconnaissance forces, the company's reconnoitering mission is resumed.

■ 134. DISPOSITIONS DURING APPROACH TO COMBAT.—Dispositions of the company depend upon missions received and the situation. The following dispositions are appropriate for a reconnaissance company preceding the battalion on a sudden march to battle and charged initially only with reconnaissance missions:

a. When the battalion marches on a single road a reconnaissance platoon reconnoiters the main axis, preferably several miles in advance of the rest of the company. It will usually be desirable to employ a second reconnaissance platoon on patrol missions to the flanks of the main axis. Reconnaissance company headquarters with the third reconnaissance platoon and the pioneer platoon move along the main axis.

b. When the battalion moves on two roads one reconnaissance platoon reconnoiters each road and the contiguous terrain. Company headquarters and the pioneer platoon move on the road which seems most important. The remaining reconnaissance platoon accompanies company headquarters or is detached on special missions.

c. When the battalion moves on three roads, one reconnaissance platoon reconnoiters each road. In some cases they may be attached to tank destroyer companies. The company commander and the pioneer platoon usually move along the central route.

■ 135. COMBAT.—a. When the tank destroyer companies become engaged with the enemy, the reconnaissance company elements break off frontal contact, and unless assigned other missions move to the flanks. The battalion commander usually assigns missions to the reconnaissance company by radio; at times this will be after combat is engaged. Such missions may be—

(1) Further reconnaissance.
(2) Flank security.
(3) Liaison with other units.
(4) Mopping up in rear of the battalion.
(5) Reconnoitering or blocking the enemy's retreat.
(6) Keeping open a route for supply vehicles.
(7) Acting as mobile reserve for the battalion.

b. If the battalion retires before a superior armored force, elements of the reconnaissance company assist in covering the withdrawal by delaying and harassing actions. In such a situation the pioneer platoon erects road blocks and obstacles and places antitank mines and demolitions. The reconnaissance platoons ambush hostile parties and confuse and blind the opposing forces by smoke screens.

■ **136. NIGHT ATTACKS.**—The reconnaissance company is especially trained to make night attacks on tanks in bivouac or "harbors." Tactics on night attacks are set forth in chapter 10.

■ **137. SECURITY MISSIONS.**—*a.* Security missions are usually executed by platoon; the company commander exercises such control as is necessary.

b. When not in the immediate presence of the enemy, the reconnaissance company ordinarily bivouacs with the remainder of the battalion, usually being located near the principal route of egress from the position. It establishes local security in the same manner as tank destroyer companies and may be required to furnish one or more outguards.

c. The reconnaissance company may be called upon to assist, with a portion of its elements, in covering the movement of the battalion into an assembly position in preparation for combat. It uses its available reserve to establish delaying groups covering the principal routes leading into the area. Duration of this mission is usually short.

CHAPTER 6

HEADQUARTERS COMPANY

■ 138. COMPOSITION.—The headquarters company consists of a company headquarters and the communication, staff, motor maintenance, and transportation platoons. For details of the organization, see T/O 18-26.

■ 139. COMPANY HEADQUARTERS.—*a.* The headquarters section is composed of the company commander, his executive, and certain enlisted men to maintain the supply, mess, and administration of the company. The motorcycle scouts are usually employed at the battalion command post for convoy control, scouting and patrolling, and as messengers. In combat, company headquarters remains with the rear echelon.

b. The motor maintenance section is responsible for second echelon maintenance of all headquarters company vehicles. It works and marches with the transportation platoon under the transportation officer.

■ 140. COMMUNICATION PLATOON.—The duties of certain members of the communication platoon are as follows:

a. Platoon leader.—For duties of the platoon leader, see paragraph 159.

b. Platoon sergeant.—(1) He assists the communication officer.

(2) In combat, he usually remains with the battalion command post.

c. Message center sergeant.—He organizes, establishes, and operates the battalion message center. As a guide for operation, see FM 24-5.

d. Radio sergeant.—(1) He is in charge of the radio section.

(2) He usually remains with the battalion command post.

(3) He supervises the operation and shifts of the radio operator.

(4) He supervises radio repair and assists the communication officer in the inspection of all of the battalion radios.

e. Radio electrician.—(1) He repairs and maintains all

73

radios within the company and, if desirable, assists in the repair of other radios in the battalion.

(2) If desirable, he assists the communication officer in the inspection of radios.

(3) He usually remains at the company command post.

f. Radio operators.—(1) They operate radios and maintain logs as prescribed in FM 24–5 and TM 11–454.

(2) They keep their sets clean, tighten all exterior connections, and report to the radio sergeant all indications of malfunctioning.

g. Panel and code corporal.—(1) He assists the message center sergeant.

(2) He encodes and decodes, or supervises the encoding and decoding of, all messages that require such action.

(3) He operates the panel station, assisted by other members of the message center section.

■ 141. Duties of Staff Platoon Noncommissioned Officers.—*a. Battalion sergeant major.*—(1) He assists S–1.

(2) In combat, he remains at the battalion command post.

(3) He receives incoming messages from the message center and distributes them to the proper staff officers.

(4) He keeps the unit journal, under supervision of S–1.

b. Personnel sergeant.—(1) He assists the personnel officer.

(2) In combat, he remains with the rear echelon.

c. Intelligence and operations sergeant.—(1) He assists S–3.

(2) In combat, he accompanies S–3, and maintains the battalion situation map and such informal records as directed by S–3.

(3) When practicable, he contacts the intelligence sergeant and checks to see that the two situation maps agree.

d. Intelligence sergeant.—(1) He assists S–2.

(2) In combat, he accompanies S–2, and maintains a situation map and such informal records as directed by S–2.

(3) When practicable, he contacts the intelligence and operations sergeant and checks to see that his situation map agrees with the battalion map.

e. Battalion supply sergeant and assistant supply sergeant.—(1) They assist S–4.

(2) In combat, they usually remain with the rear echelon.

f. Ammunition sergeant.—(1) He assists S–4 and the battalion supply sergeant in ammunition supply functions.

(2) In combat, he usually remains with the rear echelon.

■ **142. MOTOR MAINTENANCE PLATOON.**—*a.* For duties of the platoon leader, see paragraph 161.

b. The motor maintenance platoon performs second echelon maintenance as prescribed in FM 25–10 and AR 850–15. In combat, every possible expedient will be used to repair vehicles; it is a point of honor with maintenance personnel to keep vehicles rolling.

c. During combat, the motor maintenance platoon is divided into two echelons. One part remains with the rear echelon. The other part, including the wrecker, follows the combat echelon; upon deployment, this forward maintenance echelon reports to the battalion command post and operates from there as required.

d. The motor maintenance platoon assists in operating the vehicle recovery service. (See par. 56.)

■ **143. TRANSPORTATION PLATOON.**—*a.* For duties of the platoon leader, see paragraph 162.

b. The transportation platoon contains the vehicles required for the battalion baggage and kitchens, and for the supply of rations, water, ammunition, gasoline, and oil. The transportation platoon operates from the rear echelon, carrying ammunition and other supplies to the combat echelon as required.

c. Refueling in the field is effected by vehicles of the fuel section moving along march units and exchanging full cans for empty ones. When it is impracticable for fuel vehicles to move along a column, they leave filled cans at a designated rendezvous where companies send their empty cans. Upon conclusion of a march or day's operation, refueling is effected before drivers rest. Morning finds every vehicle completely refueled.

d. The ammunition vehicles, in combat, report to the location designated for the battalion ammunition distributing point. The ammunition section keeps is vehicles loaded with the required types of ammunition by a shuttle service back to an ammunition distributing point designated by higher authority.

75

■ 144. DISPOSITION OF COMPANY.—*a.* *On the march.*—The communication platoon and a portion of the staff platoon move with the combat echelon. The remainder of the company moves with the battalion rear echelon under the headquarters company commander.

b. Bivouac.—When the battalion is in a bivouac, headquarters company is in the center protected by the tank destroyer companies. A plan of defense of the bivouac in case of surprise attack will be drawn up for each element of headquarters company, and all personnel will be assigned duties protecting specified areas.

c. Action during combat.—When the battalion enters combat, the rear echelon remains in concealment. As soon as the combat echelon leaves the bivouac, the commander of headquarters company causes each company supply sergeant to report to him and gives them instructions in regard to the regrouping of all rear echelon establishments. For purposes of control and security these are concentrated in a central location, usually that of headquarters company. All-around protection is established. Motorcycle scouts are sent to critical points to give warning of hostile attack. Machine guns on vehicles are prepared for action; they may be placed on ground mounts covering critical points.

d. Return of combat echelon.—In case the headquarters company commander is notified that the combat echelon is returning to the bivouac, he causes the rear echelon personnel and vehicles of the various companies to resume their former positions shortly before arrival of the destroyer units.

CHAPTER 7

MEDICAL DETACHMENT

■ 145. ORGANIZATION.—a. Medical service for the tank destroyer battalion is provided by a medical detachment. During active operations, this detachment is divided into company aid groups, the battalion aid station group, and the rear echelon group. One company aid man or technician should be assigned to each platoon of the tank destroyer companies and to each reconnaissance platoon of the reconnaissance company. One or two technicians should be assigned to the rear echelon. The remainder of the enlisted men remain with the battalion aid station. Usually all medical officers are with the battalion aid station; if three officers are available, one may remain with the rear echelon. (See FM 8–5.)

b. The medical detachment is equipped with its own motor transportation, driven and maintained (first echelon maintenance) by its own personnel. Second echelon maintenance, fuel, and lubricants are furnished by the tank destroyer battalion.

c. The detachment does not have a mess; its members are rationed with the companies of the battalion according to convenience.

d. Equipment and supplies for the battalions, except emergency medical, are procured in the usual manner through S–4.

CHAPTER 8

TANK DESTROYER BATTALION

SECTION I

BATTALION HEADQUARTERS

■ 146. COMPOSITION.—A tank destroyer battalion consists of a headquarters and headquarters company, a reconnaissance company, three destroyer companies, and a medical detachment. For details of organization, see T/O 18–25.

■ 147. BATTALION COMMANDER.—*a. General.*—(1) The battalion commander personally controls the battalion and is responsible for its condition and operations. His professional knowledge must include a thorough understanding of the combat and service elements in the battalion and of their tactical and technical employment, and a general understanding of the employment, limitations, and capabilities of units of other arms that may be associated with the battalion in combat.

(2) In preparation for combat, the mission of the battalion commander is to bring his unit to a high state of training and combat proficiency. In carrying out this training mission he subordinates administration to training, and thus insures that the training for combat of individuals and small units is a continuing process. He promotes group feeling within the battalion and cooperative action among its various parts. He encourages initiative, ingenuity, and aggressiveness throughout all echelons of the battalion. Having indicated his policies and given his directives, he allows his staff and subordinates the maximum freedom of action in order to foster self-reliance and initiative.

b. Exercise of command.—Whenever the situation requires, the battalion commander obtains the views of his staff officers and principal subordinates before he announces his decisions and issues his orders. However, he alone is responsible for what his unit does or fails to do.

c. Relations with staff.—(1) The battalion commander is provided with a staff to relieve him of the details of planning and administration; to act as his agents in coordinating the plans and operations of the various units and services under his command; to prepare detailed orders for the execution of his plans; and to assist him in supervising the execution of these orders.

(2) He encourages his staff officers to submit suggestions and recommendations. He supports the action taken by staff officers in carrying out his directives and policies. However, he does not hesitate to correct them and rectify their mistakes.

(3) The commander inspires the utmost efforts from his staff. He causes staff work to be properly organized, distributed, and simplified in order that excessive strain will not be placed upon individuals.

d. Relations with subordinate commanders and troops.—The relations of the battalion commander with the commanders of subordinate units are similar to the relations maintained with the staff. He spends considerable time with his unit commanders and their men. He makes inspections and informal visits during which he talks to individuals and to groups. During combat such visits promote confidence, respect, and loyalty. They give the commander first-hand knowledge of the tactical situation and of the needs and capabilities of his units. In issuing instructions, however, the battalion commander does not interfere with the command responsibilities of his subordinates except in emergencies. (See FM 21–50 and FM 100–5.)

e. Conduct in battle.—(1) In combat, the battalion commander, personally and through his staff, provides for reconnaissance and security, liaison with higher headquarters and adjacent units, timely dissemination of information and orders, coordination of effort and cooperation by all units, and replacement of personnel and supplies.

(2) With the assistance of his staff, he studies possible contingencies and formulates tentative plans to meet them. So far as practicable, he makes these tentative plans known to subordinate commanders.

(3) During combat, it is essential that the battalion commander make reconnaissance, visit his subordinate comman-

ders and troops, and move where he can best control the action of his battalion. His party usually accompanies him. (See par. 150b(2).) He keeps in contact with his subordinate commanders, command post, higher headquarters, and sometimes observation aviation, by radio or other available means of communication.

■ 148. STAFF.—*a*. The battalion staff includes the unit staff, special staff, and liaison officers.

b. The unit staff consists of—
    Executive.
    Adjutant (S–1) and assistant adjutant (personnel officer).
    Intelligence officer (S–2).
    Plans and training officer (S–3).
    Supply officer (S–4).

c. The special staff includes those officers who by their assignments are considered as members of the special staff. They are—
    Communication officer (platoon leader, communication platoon, headquarters company).
    Gas officer.
    Motor officer (platoon leader, motor maintenance platoon, headquarters company).
    Surgeon (commanding medical detachment).

■ 149. STAFF TEAM.—*a*. The unit staff is so organized that it can function continuously, day and night, throughout an operation. It is organized into two groups, each group capable of functioning while the other group rests.

b. Each member of the unit staff must be trained to take over the duties of any other member. This is essential in order to organize the staff for continuous operation and to replace staff officers who become casualties or leave the command post for reconnaissance and visits.

■ 150. STAFF ECHELONS.—*a*. During combat, and during movements immediately preceding combat, the battalion headquarters usually is divided into a forward and rear echelon. The forward echelon is known as the *command post*. That part of headquarters that remains in rear is known as the *rear echelon*. (See FM 100–5.)

b. (1) The following usually constitute the command post personnel:

Battalion commander.

Executive.

Adjutant.

Intelligence officer.

Plans and training officer.

Communication officer.

Surgeon.

Organic liaison officers when not on duty at other command posts.

Liaison officers from other units.

Enlisted assistants to the above, radio operators.

Message center personnel, messengers, and drivers.

(2) The battalion commander's party usually consists of the commanding officers, S–2, S–3, an assistant S–3 if available, intelligence and operation sergeants, necessary clerks, radio operators, drivers, messengers, and sometimes a small security detachment. The party has no fixed station.

c. An assistant surgeon, together with the majority of the enlisted personnel of the medical detachment, although not part of the command post personnel, remain near the command post after deployment of the battalion. (See par. 145.)

d. (1) The following personnel usually remain at the rear echelon:

Company commander, headquarters company.

Personnel officer.

Enlisted members of the supply and administrative sections.

A small number of the enlisted men of the medical detachment.

(2) If three medical officers are with the battalion medical detachment, one may remain with the rear echelon.

e. The supply officer does not necessarily remain with the rear echelon; he goes where he can best perform his duties.

f. The battalion motor officer, initially, remains with the rear echelon. The necessity for supervising vehicle recovery will often require him to move forward. (See par. 56.)

■ 151. STAFF OFFICER.—*a.* A staff officer, as such, has no authority to command. (See FM 101–5.) Whenever a staff officer issues an order it is only to transmit the orders or desires of the commander. If a staff officer deems it advisable to issue an order which is not in furtherance of an announced policy and has not been specifically authorized by his commander, he must inform his commander without delay of its content.

b. The staff secures and furnishes such information as may be required by the commander, prepares the details of his plan, translates his decision and plan into orders, and causes such orders to be transmitted to the troops. It brings to the commander's attention matters which require his action or about which he should be informed, makes a continuous study of the situation, and prepares tentative plans for possible future contingencies for the consideration of the commander. Within the scope of its authority, it supervises the execution of plans and orders and takes such other action as is necessary to carry out the commander's intentions.

c. The staff officer should have a thorough knowledge of the policies of his commander and should be acquainted with subordinate commanders and their units. A staff officer should be an active, well-informed assistant to the commander and a helpful adviser to subordinate commanders.

■ 152. BATTALION EXECUTIVE.—a. The battalion executive is the principal assistant to the battalion commander. In the temporary absence of the commander, he makes such decisions as the occasion demands, based on the known wishes and policies of the commander. He keeps abreast of the situation and is familiar with the commander's plans. The executive usually remains at the command post. If he leaves the command post, he designates the next senior member of the unit staff to perform his duties.

b. The executive performs those duties delegated to him by the commander, and in general those outlined for the chief of staff in FM 101–5. He adapts himself to the role assigned him by his particular commander. He relieves the commander of details, particularly those of an administrative nature. He sees that the commander is kept informed of matters pertaining to the strength, morale, organization, training, equipment, supply of the battalion, and the tactical situation. He brings to the commander's attention matters requiring correction. He presents facts concisely with recommendations. He amplifies decisions made by the commander.

c. The executive coordinates the activities of the staff. He sees that its members cooperate and exchange information. He transmits the instructions and decisions of the commander; he examines the reports, plans, and orders prepared by members of the staff for corrections, completeness, clarity, and brevity; he causes staff officers to verify the execution of orders, and he supervises the keeping of the unit situation map.

■ 153. ADJUTANT (S–1).—a. The adjutant performs duties similar to those outlined in FM 101–5 for the adjutant general and for the G–1, excluding duties inapplicable to the battalion or charged to the personnel officer. The combat duties of the adjutant include—

(1) Supervision of the training and functioning of the administrative section, staff platoon.

(2) Replacements of personnel and arrangements for receiving, processing, assigning, and quartering.

(3) Recreation and morale; supervision of religious, recreational, and welfare matters and other nonmilitary agencies.

(4) Decorations, citations, honors, and awards.

(5) Strength reports, casualty reports, prisoners of war reports, reports relative to enemy civilians (when applicable).

(6) Maintaining the unit journal.

(7) Command post arrangements, including allotting of space; supervision of movements of the command post and its security and concealment when the command post and rear echelon are separated.

(8) Allotment of space or areas for camps, bivouacs, or other quarters of the battalion.

(9) Supervision of mail clerks, mail distribution and collection.

(10) Composition of quartering parties, their time and place of reporting, rations and equipment to be taken, and arrangements for occupying selected sites.

(11) Custody and evacuation of prisoners of war. (Coordination with S–2.)

b. S–1 visits companies, whenever necessary, to obtain information as to casualties, replacements required, and actual strength of units; obtains data relating to the foregoing from S–3 and S–2; keeps commander informed of the strength of the command.

c. S–1 keeps in touch with the tactical situation and the activities of other staff officers and is prepared to take over their duties when necessary.

■ 154. INTELLIGENCE OFFICER (S–2).—*a. References.*—For doctrines governing combat intelligence, see FM 100–5; for the general considerations and special aspects of combat intelligence, see FM 30–5; and for counterintelligence, see FM 30–25. For special subjects pertinent to intelligence, see other Field Manuals of the 30-series.

b. Essential elements of information.—FM 30–5 lists essential elements of information pertinent to all collecting agencies. The following are essential elements that are particularly applicable to tank destroyer units:

(1) In an advance by the enemy, the number, strength, composition, and direction of movement of armored columns and the probable place of contact.

(2) In an attack by the enemy, the direction and weight of the main tank attack and the location and composition of other hostile elements that might prevent the tank destroyers from reaching the tanks.

(3) In a defense by the enemy, the locations and composition of armored forces and their capabilities for counterattack.

(4) In an enemy retrograde movement, the direction of movement and location of demolitions and defensive positions; the locations and dispositions of the hostile armored forces.

(5) In a pursuit by an enemy, the strength, composition, location, and direction of movement of armored and other encircling or enveloping forces and where they will make contact; the location and composition of armored forces capable of pursuing by direct pressure.

(6) In projected operations, the nature, location, and condition of natural and man-made obstacles to our maneuver, and the determination of important terrain features not shown on available maps.

c. Information not limited to essential elements.—The essential elements of information are guides governing the search for information and not limitations regulating the information to be reported. Therefore, collecting agencies will transmit all enemy information which comes to their attention.

d. Duties.—The duties of the intelligence officer are—

(1) Special training of battalion intelligence personnel, and such supervision of intelligence and counterintelligence instruction within the battalion as directed by the battalion commander.

(2) Supervision of the training and functioning of that part of the operations and intelligence section, staff platoon, assigned to him.

(3) Through S–3, preparation of intelligence plans and orders to information collecting agencies.

(4) Maintenance of liaison and exchange of information with intelligence agencies of subordinate, higher, and neighboring units.

(5) Recording, evaluating, and interpreting information; and distributing information and military intelligence to the commander, interested staff officers, and higher, subordinate, and neighboring units.

(6) Examination of enemy personnel and captured documents and material for information of immediate importance to the battalion.

(7) Procurement and issue of maps, aerial photographs, and photomaps.

(8) General supervision of counterintelligence measures within the battalion.

■ 155. PLANS AND TRAINING OFFICER (S–3).—*a.* S–3 is concerned primarily with the training and tactical operations of the battalion.

b. The duties of S–3 include—

(1) Supervision of the training and functioning of that part of the operations and intelligence section, staff platoon, assigned to him.

(2) Assembly of facts to assist the commander in his estimate of the training situation.

(3) Formulation of training plans in accordance with the commander's directive.

(4) Planning for, and supervision and coordination of—

(a) Allocation and use of training facilities.

(b) Organization and conduct of battalion schools.

(c) Allocation of equipment (with S–4).

(d) Assignment of replacements (with S–1).

(e) Troop movements (with S–4 on transportation and supply).

(f) Distribution of troops in bivouac, assembly areas, and in combat (with staff officers concerned).

(g) Reconnaissance and security measures (with S–2).

(5) Training records and reports of training.

(6) Study of the tactical situation and preparation of tactical plans (with S–2 and S–4).

(7) Preparation of field orders and operation maps (with other staff officers).

(8) Liaison with higher, adjacent, and subordinate units.

(9) Personal transmission by radio during combat of such orders as the battalion commander directs.

(10) Posting of S–3 data on the situation map.

(11) Tactical reports required by the executive.

(12) Signal communication and advance planning for special signal measures. (See also FM 101–5.)

■ 156. SUPPLY OFFICER (S–4).—a. The supply officer supervises the battalion supply service and is responsible for its functioning in accordance with orders and with the tactical plan of the battalion; keeps in touch with S–3 and the tactical situation, with the headquarters and headquarters company, with subordinate commanders and the troops, with G–4 of the higher headquarters, and with all supply installations.

b. S–4 supervises the training and operation of the members of the supply section of the staff platoon.

c. The duties of S–4 include planning for and supervision of—

(1) Procurement, storage, transportation, and distribution of all supplies except emergency medical.

(2) Location of supply and maintenance installations.

(3) Maintenance of equipment.

(4) Salvage as directed.

(5) Collection and disposal of captured supplies (with S–2 for examination of material and with G–4 of higher headquarters for disposition).

(6) Evacuation.

(7) Traffic control (with S-3).

(8) Recommendations concerning protection of the battalion train bivouac and other rear area installations (with S-3 and headquarters commandant).

(9) Property responsibility and accountability.

(10) Administrative orders and supply arrangements of higher authority.

(11) Procurement of ammunition and other class V items such as pyrotechnics, antitank mines, and chemicals, and distribution to companies.

(12) Establishment, operation, and movement of the battalion ammunition distributing point.

(13 Ammunition needs of subordinate units.

(14) Preparation of ammunition records and reports.

(15) Control of elements of the battalion ammunition train not released to lower units.

■ 157. PERSONNEL OFFICER.—*a.* The personnel officer is designated as assistant adjutant.

b. The personnel officer heads the personnel officer's group of the S-1 section. This group includes the personnel sergeant and designated clerks from the administrative section, headquarters company; it may include one clerk from each company of the battalion. It maintains the company and battalion records, reports, rosters, returns, files, and correspondence prescribed by AR 345-5.

c. In general, the personnel officer is charged with the preparation, maintenance, and safekeeping of all records, documents, correspondence, and statistics of a personnel and administrative nature that are not required to be kept at the command posts of the companies or the battalions. (See AR 345-5.) He is responsible under the adjutant for the administration of all company and detachment personnel records of which the battalion adjutant is custodian. (These do not include basic company records retained by the company commanders.) (See AR 345-5.) He is charged with the custody of company funds when the companies go into combat, or when, in the opinion of the battalion commander, funds might be lost because of casualties. He receipts for the funds and for all papers pertaining to them. He has no authority to make disbursements and returns the funds to the permanent custodians when the situation permits. (See TM 12–250.) He is also charged with the training of personnel to replace clerks with the battalion staff.

■ 158. COMPANY COMMANDER, HEADQUARTERS COMPANY.—*a.* The company commander, headquarters company, acts as headquarters commandant when the command post and rear echelon are together. His duties as headquarters commandant are—

(1) Acting as quartering officer under, or in place of, S–1.

(2) Supervision of the physical movement of the command post, and furnishing the necessary men and transportation from company headquarters.

(3) Supervision of the messing and quartering of command post personnel.

b. When the command post and rear echelon are separated, the company commander, headquarters company, is responsible for the rear echelon. His duties include—

(1) Arrangement, installation, and movement of the rear echelon.

(2) Provision for the security of the rear echelon, using available personnel.

(3) Provision for the concealment of the rear echelon from air observation.

(4) Assistance to S–4 in the delivery of supplies to the combat echelon. When delivery is particularly difficult or important, he may direct his executive officer to accompany and take charge of the delivering party.

■ 159. COMMUNICATION OFFICER.—*a.* The commander of the communication platoon is the battalion communication officer. As a special staff officer he is adviser to the battalion commander and staff on matters of signal communication technique.

b. In addition to commanding the communication platoon, his duties are:

(1) Such supervision of the technical training of communication personnel throughout the battalion as may be delegated to him by the commander.

(2) Technical advice and assistance to S–4 regarding the supply of signal communication material for the battalion.

(3) Plans and recommendations for establishing a system of radio nets throughout the battalion during combat, and technical supervision of the system to insure maximum coordination within the battalion and between it and the systems of adjacent, supporting, attached, and higher units. (See par. 166.)

(4) In combat, preparing or securing from higher headquarters such orders and signal operation instructions as may be needed to insure tactical and technical control of the signal communication system of his unit; distribution of such orders and signal operation instructions throughout his unit.

(5) Recommendations for procurement and replacement of signal communication personnel.

■ 160. GAS OFFICER.—*a.* The battalion gas officer is selected by the battalion commander; he performs his duties as gas officer in addition to his other duties.

b. His duties are—

(1) Recommendations to S–4 concerning the supply of chemical munitions and antichemical protective equipment.

(2) Supervision and coordination of gas defense training in the battalion and periodic inspections of gas defense equipment.

(3) Supervision of the installation and maintenance of gas defense measures.

(4) Supervision of the use of decontaminating agents.

(5) Recommendations concerning the use of chemicals and smoke.

(6) Recommendations for standing orders concerning gas defense measures.

(7) Study of types and characteristics of chemicals and chemical equipment used by the enemy, and methods of employing them.

■ 161. MOTOR OFFICER.—*a.* Motor operations and maintenance are functions of command. Continuous and efficient operations require that all command personnel give to maintenance activities the necessary time and effort to obtain desired results. Although a battalion commander may properly delegate authority to his subordinates, considerable personal and active control on the part of the commander is

89

necessary to maintain vehicles in a high state of operating efficiency.

b. The commander of the motor maintenance platoon is the battalion motor officer. He must be qualified through training and experience to supervise motor maintenance operations and to advise his superiors and company commanders regarding maintenance measures and the condition of vehicles within the battalion.

c. In addition to commanding the motor maintenance platoon, his duties are—

(1) As directed by the battalion commander supervision of the maintenance of all vehicles within the battalion.

(2) Informing the battalion commander of the maintenance conditions within the battalion.

(3) Supervision of the recovery system. (See par. 56.)

(4) Recommendations to S–4 for the procurement of spare parts.

■ 162. TRANSPORTATION OFFICER.—*a.* The battalion transportation officer commands the transportation platoon.

b. In addition to commanding the platoon, his duties are—

(1) Supervision of the maintenance and operation of all headquarters and headquarters company and attached vehicles.

(2) To keep S–3 and S–4 informed as to the status of all transportation platoon and attached vehicles.

■ 163. SURGEON.—*a.* The battalion surgeon commands the medical detachment. He advises the battalion commander and staff on all matters pertaining to the health of the command and the sanitation of the battalion area; the training of all troops in military sanitation and first aid; the location and operation of medical establishments and the evacuation service.

b. The surgeon performs the following duties in addition to commanding the medical detachment:

(1) He supervises the instruction of the battalion in personal hygiene, military sanitation, and first aid.

(2) He makes medical and sanitary inspections and keeps the battalion commander informed of the medical situation in the battalion.

(3) He establishes and operates the battalion dispensary.

(4) He requisitions for medical and dental supplies and equipment required by the medical detachment.

(5) He arranges with the division surgeon for the evacuation of casualties from aid stations.

(6) He supervises the collection and evacuation of wounded.

(7) He supervises the preparation of casualty lists and other required records pertaining to the medical service.

c. Detailed duties of the surgeon are contained in Army Regulations and in FM 8-10.

■ 164. LIAISON OFFICER.—a. Liaison officers are officers sent to or received from other units for the purpose of promoting cooperation and coordination by personal contact. (See par. 23.)

b. A liaison officer represents his commander at the command post to which he is sent. For detailed duties, see FM 101-5.

■ 165. COMMAND POST OPERATION.—a. The command post is organized for continuous operation and to insure the necessary rest for personnel. Staff officers relieve each other and the battalion commander as necessary. Enlisted personnel work in shifts.

b. All incoming messages, except those radio or telephone messages that are transmitted directly to the recipient, go first to the message center. If in code, they are then decoded. The message center sends each message to the sergeant major, who supervises its delivery to the addressee, its circulation to interested staff officers, and its return for entry in the unit journal. Staff officers mark on the message any action taken.

c. Outgoing written messages are usually sent through the message center. After the message center chief receives notice that the message has been delivered, he places the duplicate copy in his dead file for entry in the unit journal.

d. Each officer is responsible that a synopsis of each important message or order sent out or received by him orally, or by telephone or radiotelephone, is sent to the unit journal.

■ 166. RADIO NET.—a. The battalion radio net is organized so as to make the most efficient use of available sets. Details of net organization may vary from day to day. When both

91

AM and FM sets are used by the battalion, extremely careful coordination is required to obtain the best results. .

b. Organization should be such that the battalion commander, with a small party, can go where he pleases in the battalion area and still have control of his unit. It is desirable that both the commander and the executive, who usually remains at the command post when the battalion commander is absent, have radio communication with subordinate and all important agencies.

c. The battalion commander's radio usually is on the battalion command channel; radios in vehicles accompanying him should be on frequencies permitting them to receive information from airplanes and from higher headquarters. A radio on the frequency of the reconnaissance company is advantageous. Vehicles in the battalion commander's party, when practicable, contain sets facilitating intervehicle communication. When such sets are lacking, this communication is by physical contact. It is desirable for the battalion commander's party to have several channels of communication with the battalion command post.

d. The command post, when sufficient sets are available, should be able to communicate with all sets in the battalion command net, higher headquarters, the battalion rear echelon, and aviation. Sufficient sets must be provided to fulfill the battalion's responsibilities in the warning system prescribed by higher headquarters.

e. It is advantageous for liaison officers to be on the command net, thereby keeping thoroughly informed concerning the situation; however, their distance from the battalion may require the use of another set or frequency.

f. Communication with higher headquarters, aviation, the rear echelon, staff or liaison officers sent on distant missions, and at times with the reconnaissance company or a detached tank destroyer company may require long range sets capable of code operations. Long range sets probably will be required in the warning service.

g. Organization of radio nets should be such that a few vehicle casualties will not disrupt communication. Duplication of sets on important channels, or retention of a radio reserve by the battalion, is highly desirable when sufficient sets are available.

■ **167. STANDING OPERATING PROCEDURE.**—*a.* Standing operating procedure is procedure prescribed to be carried out in the absence of orders to the contrary. In the standing operating procedure of a unit are included standing procedures for those tactical and administrative features of operations that lend themselves to routine or standardized procedure without loss of effectiveness. A standing operating procedure helps to simplify and abbreviate combat orders, expedite operations, and promote teamwork. It is published as an order and governs except when specified otherwise.

b. Each battalion develops its own standing operating procedure conforming to that established by the next higher unit. In effect, the standing operating procedure of a battalion is largely an outgrowth of its training as a team combined with the policies and methods of its commander and of the next higher commander. To be effective, it must be revised periodically.

c. Speed of movement in modern warfare demands a high degree of flexibility and initiative to meet rapidly changing situations, and a commander must not permit a standing operating procedure to narrow the scope of training or destroy opportunities for the use of initiative.

SECTION II

OPERATIONS

■ **168. GENERAL.**—*a.* The ideal entry into combat is that in which sufficient time and information of the enemy and the terrain are available to commanders to insure detailed reconnaissance of the area of contemplated operations. Time allowance in the planning of moves under battle conditions must be extremely generous; failure to do so lessens the chances of successful operation. However, combat units must be trained to operate with little time for advance preparation.

b. When the battalion engages hostile tanks, it will endeavor to hem them in with surprise gun fire. Maneuver should be directed against the front, flanks, or rear in such a manner that fire superiority is gained at each point of contact. Unduly wide dispersion and loss of control of companies must be avoided when operating against massed tank attacks; wide dispersion and actions by individual companies is permissible only when operating against dispersed armored forces. The duration of the action from any one position must be violent and brief. Every opportunity is sought to take advantage of the superior mobility of tank destroyers for executing the maximum damage against hostile tanks without receiving prohibitive losses.

c. Vulnerability of the tank destroyer battalion to the action of hostile infantry renders close support by friendly foot troops highly desirable. The strength of the supporting infantry that is available will influence the method of employment of the tank destroyer battalion and the directions from which attack can be made. When hostile infantry and artillery prevent the battalion from engaging the enemy's tanks, the battalion maintains contact with the hostile covering force by patrols, the bulk of the destroyers being kept in rear. In case the hostile infantry precedes the armored elements, the battalion fights a delaying action to hold the enemy's progress to the rate of foot troops; successive ambushes are employed if the enemy engages his armored elements. When only weak forces of infantry cover the hostile tanks, the battalion evades them or defeats them by the use of reconnaissance company personnel and security elements of tank destroyer companies.

■ 169. COOPERATION WITH AVIATION.—It is essential that the tank destroyer battalion have the assistance of observation aviation for reconnaissance and liaison. This demands close cooperation between tank destroyer and air corps personnel. Air reconnaissance is particularly valuable to tank destroyer units in planning and conducting operations, and in maintaining liaison with a supported higher unit. Air observation keeps in close touch with the command post of the tank destroyer battalion by radio, dropped messages, prearranged signals, or the air-ground liaison code. It promptly reports movements which threaten the flanks or rear of firing positions and indicates suitable objectives for tank destroyer maneuver. For details of the action of observation aviation, see FM 31–35.

■ 170. ENTERING ZONE OF OPERATIONS.—*a.* The movement is preferably so timed that the unit can arrive in its initial bivouac during darkness.

b. Upon arrival in the initial park in a combat zone, the unit commander or a liaison officer reports to the command post of the unit to which the battalion is attached. The battalion starts preparations for combat, checking and servicing equipment and reorganizing its radio nets if necessary.

■ 171. PREEMPLOYMENT PERIOD.—*a.* At the first opportunity, preemployment reconnaissance of probable combat areas and routes is begun by the reconnaissance company and designated officers. Initial reconnaissance is confined to the road net, bridge capacities, and fords in the zone of operations of the supported or higher units.

b. The battalion is kept under control and only necessary reconnaissance, supply, and administrative personnel leave the park or bivouac. All personnel are kept informed of the situation.

c. The bivouac is concealed and organized for all-around defense upon occupation. Tank destroyer companies usually will be on the perimeter of the areas, with supply and administrative installations in the center. The reconnaissance company usually will be located conveniently with respect to the principal exit from the position. Combat companies post security for the defense of their sector of the position, covering routes of approach both with tank destroyer guns and dismounted security groups. Antiaircraft sections are distributed near or on the outer perimeter of the bivouac and crews are given specific instructions concerning conditions under which fire is to be opened. The battalion commander coordinates these dispositions at the earliest practicable moment.

d. Vehicles located near main roads must be particularly well concealed. It is preferable to have no vehicles within 100 yards of main roads.

e. Preparations are made to move out of the area with minimum warning, without lights, and without recourse to an assembly on or near the route of egress. Paths for each vehicle to the nearest trail are selected, marked, and cleared when necessary.

■ 172. RECONNAISSANCE PHASE.—*a.* Only when coordinated plans for contemplated employment have been made or approved by the supported or higher commander will detailed reconnaissance be initiated. This reconnaissance, conducted from the park or bivouac area, will include routes and selection of positions.

b. When occupying a position in readiness, the battalion prepares several alternative plans. Reconnaissance for each plan is made, and tentative instructions issued as to the order of march, route, and missions for each, usually through operations maps or overlays.

■ 173. MARCH PRIOR TO DEPLOYMENT.—*a.* The battalion may march as a unit (under battalion control) in one or more columns; or the tank destroyer companies, with attached reconnaissance company elements, may move independently from the park or intermediate positions to combat areas. It is desirable to march the battalion in more than one column when parallel roads not more than 5 miles apart are available. Independent movement of companies during the predeployment stage is unusual.

b. Whenever the battalion marches as a unit, the reconnaissance company informs the battalion commander of the situation and operates so that the battalion is able to maneuver under the protection of its own screen or within an area covered by its own information-gathering agencies. The battalion commander assigns specific reconnaissance missions to the reconnaissance company, indicating the routes or areas to be reconnoitered and the time for reports. In an advance toward the enemy, phase lines may be designated, corresponding to suitable assembly or attack positions. When distant from the enemy, the first phase line usually will be an important terrain feature suitable as to distance for a march halt. On nearing the enemy, when the main body of the battalion reaches one phase line, the main body of the reconnaissance company, in principle, should be on the next phase line, with patrols reconnoitering to a still more advanced line. Battalion halts on phase lines are made only if an encounter with the enemy appears imminent, or when control over the battalion must be regained.

c. When phase lines are assigned, the reconnaissance company will report the situation to the battalion commander each time the head of the main body approaches a phase line. Negative reports will be made.

d. During the movement, the battalion commander assigns such additional reconnaissance and security missions as are necessary.

e. (1) The combat echelon usually marches in the following order when in single column:

(*a*) Reconnaissance company.

(*b*) Advance guard (usually one light tank destroyer platoon).

(*c*) Forward echelon of headquarters and headquarters company (less battalion commander's party) in the following order:

> Battalion executive.
> S–1.
> Liaison officers from other units.
> Communication officer and sergeant.
> Message center.
> Surgeon.
> Other command post vehicles.

(*d*) Tank destroyer companies (less detachments).

(*e*) Medical detachment (less rear echelon medical personnel and personnel attached to companies).

(*f*) Detachment motor maintenance platoon.

(2) Rear and flank guards are employed as required by the situation.

(3) The post of the battalion commander's party is not fixed; the commander moves where he can best direct the actions of the battalion. He will frequently follow the reconnaissance company or accompany the advance guard.

(4) Destroyer company commanders march at the head of their companies unless directed to march with the battalion command post.

f. When the battalion moves in two columns, the reconnaissance company is usually divided as indicated in paragraph 134. Two destroyer companies usually move with the battalion command post on the principal route and one destroyer company on the other.

g. Tank destroyer units should expect attack by hostile aircraft, especially dive bombers and low altitude attack planes. The destroyer company which follows the command post details antiaircraft guns to protect it.

h. The rear echelon is composed of the following:

(1) Headquarters company (less elements in combat echelon).

(2) Kitchen, gas and oil, ammunition, and supply vehicles.

(3) Battalion and company motor maintenance sections (less elements in the combat echelon).

(4) Rear echelon of the medical detachment.

i. The nature of the terrain to be traversed, distance to objective, locations of assembly positions, amount of cover and concealment, time and space factors, the situation of the enemy, and the mission determine whether any other elements accompany the combat echelon in an advance to battle. If the supply and repair echelons are left behind in the park, they must be ready to move forward. The fuel section usually follows the combat echelon into an assembly position if refueling there is probable or will be required, for example, an occupation by night preparatory to a dawn attack.

j. Fuel and ammunition sections of the battalion train are usually directed to follow the rear tank destroyer company when the combat echelon is to make a long march and when physical contact between rear and combat echelons is precarious, for example, separation by defiles that might be blocked by the enemy, activity of hostile patrols, or extreme difficulty of orientation in terrain without landmarks. For operation under desert condition, see FM 31–25.

k. When tank destroyer companies with attached reconnaissance platoons move independently from the park or intermediate position to a combat area or to a position in readiness, vehicles of the fuel and ammunition sections usually will be attached.

■ 174. DEVELOPMENT AND APPROACH MARCH.—*a.* In open terrain when approaching the enemy, tank destroyer battalions must move in open dispositions. Development distributes the companies so as to insure the battalion's readiness for action and minimizes the effects of hostile aviation and artillery fire. The battalion formation usually is dictated by the road net, except when cross country movement is feasible for considerable distances. On plains or when more than one road is available, the battalion moves on a broad front. In wooded areas the battalion usually moves in column of companies with elements adopting open dispositions when crossing large clearings.

b. The objective of the approach march is fixed in accordance with the situation and the terrain. It usually will be an assembly position designated prior to the start of the march. In some cases it will be designated as a result of developments during the movement. The tank destroyer companies when close to the enemy usually follow the reconnaissance company closely in order promptly to exploit information gathered by the company; however, the tank destroyer companies must avoid premature exposure or excessive restriction of maneuver space.

c. Terrain features of tactical importance, such as those constituting antitank obstacles, or those which give extensive views over the terrain, or those which afford concealment from air and ground observation are often selected as intermediate objectives. Stream crossings, woods, road junctions, and villages may also determine bounds of movement.

d. As the battalion approaches intermediate objectives, reports from patrols, air, and other reconnaissance agencies are received and the battalion commander determines his course of action. Arrangements must be made in advance to insure receipt of such fresh reconnaissance reports at the desired time.

e. When there is little probability of hostile artillery fire or airplane attack, deployment is delayed until a late stage of the advance.

■ 175. OCCUPATION OF ASSEMBLY POSITION.—a. Unless a tank destroyer battalion, due to a hostile advance, is already located in a suitable position from which to launch an attack, or the situation is so critical that piecemeal engagement of elements is necessary, it will usually be desirable to halt the battalion in an assembly position to regain control, especially if the unit has made a long march by night or under air attack. Halts in an assembly position for refueling are often necessary. If possible, company commanders or representatives are assembled to receive final orders in the assembly position. If cover is available and hostile air activity permits, companies halt in dispersed and concealed column off the road for a minimum time during which units complete preparation for battle.

b. Security squads protect front, flanks, and rear from being reconnoitered or attacked by hostile forces during the occupation of the assembly position. The advance guard and detachments of the reconnaissance company are employed at a greater distance to block the principal avenues of approach to the position. Other detachments of the reconnaissance company reconnoiter hostile dispositions, the probable combat area, and the routes thereto.

■ 176. ENGAGEMENTS WITH ARMORED ELEMENTS,—Engagement with hostile armored elements may occur in several ways. Examples of types of engagement are:

a. When engaging an armored force that is in movement, either in column or deployed, the battalion may send an element against the head of the hostile dispositions while other elements engage either or both flanks, or rear. The battalion frequently moves to actions of this kind from a position in readiness. Such actions usually are characterized by rapidity, and may take the form of a meeting engagement. The battalion commander insures that the deployment is initiated prior to contact.

b. The battalion may select ambush positions prior to contact. One company is usually posted to block or delay the head of the hostile force while another company engages the flank. Tank destroyer companies in this type of action initially engage the bulk of their strength. A battalion reserve, usually a company, is essential.

c. The battalion may attack tanks in parks or assembly positions.

■ 177. PLANS OF ACTION.—*a.* The amount of detail in orders will largely depend upon the time available for preparation of the operation and the degree of training of the troops.

b. When the battalion enters action from a position in readiness, it often will put into execution a prearranged plan. The attack order in such case will consist merely of "Plan 1 (or 2) ACTION."

c. When a battalion enters action directly from route column, usually only fragmentary orders assigning combat missions, given by radio, will be practicable. These may be amplified later.

d. When the situation permits occupation of an assembly position, the battalion commander completes his own reconnaissance and formulates his plan of action while the assembly position is being occupied. In accordance with his estimate of the situation and orders received from higher authority, he determines his initial dispositions and scheme of maneuver.

e. The basic battalion scheme of maneuver is always clearly indicated in the battalion commander's orders; for example, to pin the enemy against an obstacle and destroy him, to surprise him in bivouac to envelop a flank, or to draw the enemy into an ambush.

■ **178. TANK DESTROYER COMPANY MISSIONS.**—*a.* Tank destroyer companies, because of the nature of their combat, must perform a most difficult operation; this operation is maneuver against a strong force that is itself capable of rapid maneuver. Therefore, the companies usually cannot be assigned battle missions that require them to act or maneuver in a specifically described manner; battle missions must be of a general nature.

b. Attack echelon companies are given their battle tasks in terms of objectives, directions of attack, combat areas, or zones of action.

(1) *Objectives.*—In fast moving situations, units are usually assigned objectives with, at times, a general direction of advance. In most cases the designated objective of a tank destroyer unit may be any armored element appearing in a given portion of terrain. Exceptionally, a terrain feature itself may constitute an objective. Assignment of a direction of advance is not to be regarded as preventing advantageous detours; however, when a route is indicated as an axis of advance, the unit is expected to maintain sufficient force in the vicinity of the road to control it.

(2) *Direction of attack.*—When the general plan of action can be determined in advance, and the battalion commander considers it feasible closely to coordinate the start of the action, he may designate the region in which units are to form for action. They should be able to reach the designated

position without the necessity of combat.   A general direction of advance therefrom may be prescribed.   Actual initiation of the action may be effected by radio or other signal.   The method of action is left to the recipient unless otherwise stated.

(3) *Combat areas.*—Combat areas are assigned when it is necessary to act in terrain which is divided into compartments by natural obstacles hindering lateral movement or when it is desired to prescribe the exact region where subordinate units are to operate initially.   Boundaries of combat areas are indications only, and in emergencies subordinate commanders do not hesitate to disregard them so long as they do not interfere with the actions of adjacent units.   The objective of a unit which has been assigned a combat area is any hostile force encountered in or near the area.   The method of action is left entirely to the recipient of the order.   The relative size of the combat area is in accordance with the contemplated degree of control.   In cases when it is necessary to act simultaneously over an extensive region and decentralized action appears necessary, large combat areas may be assigned.

(4) *Zones of action.*—A zone of action is a special form of combat area.   It requires advance in a given direction.   Zones of action are usually assigned only if the battalion itself, acting in conjunction with other troops, has been assigned a zone of action in which to advance.   Division of the battalion zone into company zones is advisable only when the battalion frontage is large enough to require initial engagement of more than one company, and when visible landmarks clearly divide the terrain.   In other cases the formation and direction of advance are indicated, together with any necessary instructions relative to maintenance of contact.

c. When a unit occupies an ambush position, surprise mass action against the enemy is contemplated.   The initial method of action of the recipient of the order is thereby prescribed.   He may adopt another method of action only in an emergency or when the situation has developed in a manner different from that anticipated.

d. Reserve units are assigned an initial location or directed to follow a designated unit or advance along a prescribed axis.

■ 179. COORDINATION OF ACTION.—An action may be coordinated as to time by requiring units to initiate movements or cross a given line at a designated time. When the situation permits, companies may be directed to an initial location, and upon arrival directed by radio to initiate their action. When a friendly force holds a suitable line of departure, this action usually will be desirable.

■ 180. ALLOTMENT OF CHEMICAL TROOPS.—*a.* When a chemical platoon is attached, the battalion usually suballots mortars to tank destroyer companies if the latter do not have 81-mm mortars. Platoon headquarters and at least one chemical mortar are usually kept with the battalion commander.

b. The chemical platoon is employed as a unit when observation from an important terrain feature must be blinded, or when a continuous screen of smoke is required over a wide front.

■ 181. CONTROL OF ACTION.—*a.* The battalion commander and his party observe and control the conduct and progress of the action throughout, not hesitating to move to any location which facilitates this control. The party moves with wide dispersion. During the approach, the battalion commander, with a small security detachment, may be close behind the reconnaissance company or accompanying the advance guard. In an engagement, he is frequently near the tank destroyer company that is most heavily engaged or wherever he has good radio communication with all elements of the battalion and where he can observe the main features of the action.

b. In accordance with developments, the battalion commander engages reserves, alters missions, and changes combat areas. He keeps informed of the situation by reports from the engaged units, battalion reconnaissance, liaison with air and other units, and by personal observation. Radio communication and the flexibility and maneuverability of tank destroyer companies enable him to forestall or surprise the enemy. After contact with hostile armored elements, the battalion commander may assign any of a variety of missions to the reconnaissance company, as indicated in paragraph 135.

c. The battalion commander endeavors constantly to reconstitute a reserve as soon as his original reserve has been committed. The integrity of tactical units is restored as soon as practicable in all cases.

d. During combat the battalion commander keeps higher authority informed of the situation of the battalion and requests such assistance from other troops as is required. When practicable, artillery fire or action of combat aviation will be requested on suitable targets, for example an immobilized tank concentration which destroyers are unable to assail. Similarly, the battalion commander may be able to arrange for neutralization of hostile weapons hindering the maneuver of his battalion and against which tank destroyer units cannot act effectively. (See FM 31–35.)

■ 182. Pursuit.—*a.* When the battalion commander recognizes that the enemy is disorganized and retreating, he takes immediate steps to press the advantage by directing commanders of the attacking echelon to engage reserves, maintain the attack, and exert relentless pressure.

b. He employs his own reserve, usually a tank destroyer company and available elements of the reconnaissance company, in an enveloping or encircling maneuver to cut off the enemy's retreat. Double envelopment is employed when conditions permit. If the battalion commander has no reserve available for the encircling or enveloping maneuver, he may detach one or more of the engaged tank destroyer companies.

c. The mobility, fire power, and demolitions capability of the reconnaissance company are employed effectively in the encircling action. It blocks defiles on the enemy's line of retreat, disrupts traffic on main roads, seeks and reports locations and movements of hostile forces, and takes under fire hostile elements attempting to reform. It especially seeks to destroy the hostile trains.

d. The units employed in the direct pressure and in an encircling or enveloping maneuver are assigned directions, zones of action, or objectives, designed to bring the pursuit to a decisive conclusion. The unit executing the encircling or enveloping maneuver advances along roads parallel to the enemy's retreat and attempts to cut off or ambush him at defiles, bridges, and other critical points. If the enemy makes a stand, prompt measures are taken to locate a vulnerable point and to attack him.

■ 183. REORGANIZATION.—*a.* Immediately after any phase of combat, reorganization and control of the battalion and its subdivisions must be effected. In effecting reorganization of the battalion, platoons should assemble, hastily reorganize, and proceed to the company rallying position; companies then reorganize and proceed to the battalion rallying position, where the process is completed. In some situations, movements to successive rallying positions will be by infiltration of vehicles, sections, and platoons.

b. The battalion commander will designate a new battalion rallying position if the previously designated position is unsuitable.

c. Battalion rallying positions preferably are in locations occupied by friendly troops. In all cases, to preclude surprise attack, infiltration by small hostile units, or ambush, battalion rallying positions are reconnoitered and secured prior to and during occupation.

d. Upon receipt of the order to rally, the battalion executive, leaving S–1 in charge of the advance command post, immediately proceeds to the rallying position. He takes with him sufficient personnel to choose company areas and to provide for necessary reconnaissance and security. Personnel with him may come from any reserve elements in the battalion or, if none are available, from the command post personnel. When he has made a hasty reconnaissance of the position and selected company areas, he designates company guides from the personnel with him. The guides then direct companies to their proper areas as they arrive at the position.

e. Whenever practicable, the command post, less elements of the battalion commander's party, under the direction of S–1, moves to the rallying position with the nearest tank destroyer company in order to obtain as much protection as possible en route.

f. As soon as companies have occupied their areas in the battalion rallying position, company commanders will report immediately to the battalion commander, leaving reorganization of the companies under the direction of their executive officers.

■ 184. FLANK PROTECTION.—*a.* The mobility and ease of control of the tank destroyer battalion adapt it for protection of the flank of a large unit against hostile armored forces.

b. The battalion usually accomplishes this mission by successive occupation of key positions by major portions of its forces, together with vigorous reconnaissance toward the flank to be guarded. It may successively detach companies at important points and advance them so as to form a moving screen, in case it is protecting the flank of a rapidly moving unit. Separation of companies by more than 5 miles is rarely necessary or desirable. (See FM 100–5.)

■ 185. DELAYING ACTION.—The battalion may be directed to fight a delaying action pending arrival of tank destroyer reinforcements. In delaying actions the battalion usually disposes two destroyer companies abreast with the third in reserve. Wide frontages are assigned. Principal routes are covered and intervening areas are observed. The reconnaissance company reconnoiters to the flanks and obstructs main roads. Withdrawal of combat echelon companies may be simultaneous or by company, and is effected on radio orders. Light platoons cover company withdrawals. The reserve is usually deployed as a covering force and is withdrawn in turn after the combat echelon has passed. The mobility of destroyers allows them to disengage rapidly and deploy again for action within a short time at a relatively distant position. Usually the order for the withdrawal designates the initial position and the first withdrawal position; subsequent positions are designated as the action progresses. Reconnaissance for the subsequent positions and routes thereto is essential.

■ 186. SUPPORTING ACTIONS.—*a.* Special considerations governing employment of tank destroyer battalions assigned to infantry, cavalry, motorized, and armored divisions are treated in the following section.

b. The tank destroyer battalion commander must be prepared to undertake missions which will tax his ingenuity and resources. He must exert every effort to fulfill such missions, exploiting the flexibility and fire power of his command, without risking its unnecessary destruction.

c. The tank destroyer commander and liaison officers of a

battalion attached to a higher unit should be able to assist the higher commander and his staff in the selection and assignment of proper and feasible missions for the battalion.

SECTION III

SUPPORT OF DIVISIONS

■ 187. GENERAL.—*a.* Tank destroyer battalions assigned or attached to a division are employed to further the combat action of the division. Their primary mission is against hostile tanks.

b. Close liaison is maintained between the division staff and the battalion. Tentative plans for employment of the battalion are prepared well in advance. The battalion commander is kept informed of the situation at all times and the battalion is tied in to the division tank warning net.

c. Coordination with other troops of the division may include exclusive reservation of routes or the allocation of priority to the battalion on selected roads, to assure rapid entry into action of the battalion when committed.

d. In emergencies when the division commander intensifies activity to locate hostile tank concentrations and ascertain their direction of movement and strength, he may consider it necessary to assign reconnaissance or observation missions to the tank destroyer battalion to augment the efforts of observation aviation and other division intelligence agencies. The tank destroyer battalion commander, in employing portions of his reconnaissance company to execute these missions, must exercise rigid economy. He must conserve the bulk of his reconnaissance personnel for the critical period when the battalion will be committed to combat. Verification of the accuracy of initial reports of contact with hostile mechanized units is advisable; it should be recalled that tanks often form part of reconnaissance elements; moreover, hostile detachments may attempt a diversion for purposes of deception.

e. When other forces are available to meet the main hostile armored attack, a tank destroyer battalion may be employed against hostile mechanized reconnaissance. When assigned a counterreconnaissance mission, the battalion accomplishes it by offensive action, whenever practicable. When the situation requires a defensive screen, elements of the reconnaissance company, reinforced as necessary, will constitute counterreconnaissance detachments (see par. 124). The bulk of the battalion will be held in rear prepared to counterattack hostile forces penetrating the screen.

■ 188. TANK DESTROYER BATTALION ATTACHED TO INFANTRY DIVISION.—*a. General.*—(1) Tentative plans for the employment of the battalion are based upon a study of the terrain, available approaches including the road net, time and space, the mission of the division, the plan of the division commander, and other factors. The ideal to be sought is that the battalion move out within a few seconds of the decision of the division commander for its engagement in combat; that it should not be delayed or interfered with by friendly troops in its advance to contact, and that in combat it be assisted to the maximum by other troops of the division. In some cases an artillery liaison officer may be sent to the battalion.

(2) Once the main hostile tank element is located and its direction of attack determined, the division commander engages the tank destroyer battalion in accordance with prearranged plans, altered as required by the situation.

b. Offensive situation.—(1) The battalion furthers the division's attack by protecting it against tank counterattacks or by removing tank threats against its flank and rear. It usually occupies successive positions in readiness. When the battalion is with an interior division, these positions are close behind the rearmost elements of attacking infantry regiments; the forward limiting features are avoidance of exposure to observed fire and availability of lateral covered routes toward the flanks of the division. When operating with a flank division, the battalion may be echeloned on the flank, prepared to meet armored counterattacks against rear installations as well as forward elements, or held in a central position of readiness.

(2) In order to allow the uninterrupted development and continuation of the division's offensive action, the tank destroyer battalion forestalls development of hostile tank counterattacks or fends them off before they can strike friendly dispositions.

c. Defensive situation.—(1) The battalion is usually held

in a centrally located position in readiness, prepared to go to meet any armored attack threatening the flanks of the division or penetrating its organized localities. Tanks will often be engaged in the vicinity of the light artillery positions.

(2) When the probable location and direction of a tank attack can be accurately determined, tank destroyers may be used to deepen and reinforce the organic antitank defense. Units equipped with towed weapons are particularly adapted to such employment; at critical times or in areas definitely threatened by tank penetration, some self-propelled weapons may be used for this purpose. Destroyers so utilized should either be dug in and carefully camouflaged, or held in readiness under cover close behind reconnoitered positions. The rest of the battalion should be held in a position in readiness a short distance in rear, prepared to operate in the same vicinity against the flanks of a tank attack.

(3) The battalion hunts down and destroys small tank units; against a large armored force reaching the division rear area, the battalion's efforts may consist primarily of delaying action to permit the effective entry into action of reinforcing tank destroyer units. If unable to defeat the hostile tanks, the battalion seeks to delay their movement, force them toward unfavorable terrain, and canalize their movement. By repeated ambushes and delivery of accurate fire from successive positions, it maintains pressure on the tanks until arrival of reinforcing elements permits their complete destruction. The battalion fights to the end to prevent capture of vital terrain features or centers of communication which it has been ordered to defend.

d. *Pursuit.*—The battalion may move close in rear of leading elements of other friendly troops to prevent small armored elements from delaying the pursuit. It also is well suited to protect a motorized encircling force from armored attack.

e. *River crossings.*—Elements of the tank destroyer battalion are usually crossed early to provide protection against armored counterattack. When the division defends a river line, the tank destroyer battalion is held beyond the range of hostile medium artillery initially, but is engaged promptly against any hostile tanks which manage to cross. Exceptionally, opportunity may be afforded for engagement against tanks which are supporting the crossing by fire from the opposite bank.

f. Retrograde movements.—The tank destroyer battalion usually forms part of the rear guard, or when a flank is exposed, the flank guard.

g. On the march.—The battalion occupies successive positions whence it can best protect the division. Depending on the situation, this may be on an exposed flank, in rear of the central column, or with advance elements of the division. Active reconnaissance is maintained. When acting as flank guard, successive key positions, covering likely avenues of tank approach, are occupied.

h. Protection of bivouacs and assembly positions.—The battalion, with reconnaissance well out, is held in a central position in readiness.

■ 189. TANK DESTROYER BATTALION ATTACHED TO MOTORIZED DIVISION.—*a. Movements.*—The motorized division is characterized by great mobility but when in movement it is highly vulnerable to armored attack. The tank destroyer battalion should move well forward within the division's dispositions or on an exposed flank in order to stop or fend off hostile armored attacks. It may be used to assist in covering the division's assembly for action.

b. Other situations.—In offensive and defensive situations, pursuits and withdrawals, a tank destroyer battalion with a motorized division operates generally as indicated for a battalion with an infantry division.

■ 190. TANK DESTROYER BATTALION ATTACHED TO CAVALRY DIVISION.—*a. Offensive situations.*—Cavalry is usually employed in advance or on a flank when operating offensively with other ground forces. The tank destroyer battalion usually operates on or near the exposed flank of the cavalry to prevent its envelopment by hostile armored forces.

b. Defensive situations.—In defensive combat, cavalry usually employs the methods of delaying action. The tank destroyer battalion will be used to operate against the front and flanks of attacking hostile armored forces which are in pursuit, either by direct pressure or encircling action.

c. Reconnaissance and counterreconnaissance.—Cavalry employed on a reconnaissance mission will usually hold the tank destroyer battalion centrally located to counterattack hostile armored units which may be directed against the main body of the reconnaissance force. When the cavalry division executes counterreconnaissance, the tank destroyer battalion will be held available to expel armored penetrations of the counterreconnaissance screen.

■ 191. TANK DESTROYER BATTALION ATTACHED TO ARMORED DIVISION OR GHQ TANK GROUP.—*a. General.*—Tank destroyer battalions attached to armored divisions are frequently employed to protect a bivouac, assembly position, or rallying position; to guard an exposed flank, or protect the rear of the division. They may be employed in combat to fend off attacks of hostile tanks, thus allowing the armored division to concentrate its efforts on its principal mission.

b. Employment.—Tank destroyer battalions with armored divisions are not the only units fitted for offensive engagement against hostile tanks as is the case when with other types of divisions; their employment is affected by this consideration. It is marked by frequent alternation of wide deployments and assemblies in executing successive covering or protective missions.

c. March.—The battalion may be used as a unit, or companies may be attached to armored regiments or combat commands when the division moves in more than one column. During the advance tank destroyer units usually move near the head of the unit to which they are attached. The entire battalion is often used to guard an exposed flank; it is attached to or acts as flank guard.

d. Protection of bivouacs or assembly positions.—When armored units go into assembly positions, tank destroyer units immediately deploy to cover likely avenues of approach for hostile armored forces. A portion of the battalion is held in mobile reserve.

e. Protection of the rear installations.—The rear installations of the division are far more vulnerable to armored attack than the combat echelon; the tank destroyer battalion will frequently be assigned to their protection. It occupies a centrally located position in readiness and reconnoiters vigorously.

f. During combat.—(1) The tank destroyer units may advance behind the second echelon of attack, usually the second armored battalion in depth. They are prepared to repel counterattacks from flank and rear. If a flank is exposed, the battalion is located to protect it.

(2) As the attack progresses, rear tank units will pass through the tank destroyers to enter combat. After the objective is reached, the tank destroyers move forward and protect the reorganization.

(3) In defense the tank destroyer battalion as a unit is usually held in mobile reserve initially.

g. Retrograde movements and river crossings.—In retrograde movements and river crossings, employment of the battalion is generally similar to that indicated for battalions with infantry divisions.

CHAPTER 9

TANK DESTROYER GROUP

SECTION I

ORGANIZATION, FUNCTIONS, AND COMPONENTS

■ 192. TANK DESTROYER GROUP.—*a.* The tank destroyer group is a force of variable composition, organized for mass action against large armored units. It consists primarily of—

(1) A headquarters capable of maneuvering and administering a force of all arms.

(2) Several (usually three) tank destroyer battalions.

(3) Other attached troops in accordance with the situation.

b. These attached troops may include ground and air reconnaissance elements, tanks, mechanized cavalry, motorized infantry, engineers, and chemical warfare units. The tank destroyer group is preferably engaged in concert with other troops but is capable of independent action against a large armored unit.

■ 193. FUNCTIONS OF COMPONENTS.—*a.* Tank destroyer battalions constitute the major combat element of the group.

b. Observation aviation and the warning service furnish information of the approach of hostile armored units.

c. Attached mechanized cavalry furnishes distant ground reconnaissance and provides a major contribution to the warning service of the group. It gains and maintains contact with hostile armored units and furnishes information of their activities and those of friendly troops engaged against the enemy, as well as information of the terrain.

d. Attached motorized infantry constitutes the group's principal means of action against hostile foot troops. It protects tank destroyer units against infantry attack. By defeating foot troops protecting hostile tanks in bivouacs or assembly areas, it allows destroyers to engage the latter.

When hostile infantry is in superior strength, it maintains contact and forces the enemy to commit his tanks to action or to be constrained to move only at the rate of foot troops.

e. Tanks provide the group with means of clearing up vague situations rapidly, and for prompt offensive action against small forces of hostile foot troops. Tanks assist in the rapid penetration of screens providing security for hostile tank assemblies. During combat against armored forces, they constitute a mobile reserve.

f. Attached antiaircraft elements are used on the march and in bivouac to protect the group command post and units which contain few or no organic antiaircraft weapons. In combat they protect vital areas against hostile air attack, and as a secondary mission engage hostile tanks.

g. Attached engineers lay mines and obstruct routes so as to canalize or impede the movements of hostile armored forces, and assist the rapid movement of the tank destroyer group.

h. Attached chemical troops screen the movements of destroyers with smoke, cover withdrawals by blinding hostile observation, and assist in canalizing hostile movements.

Section II

TACTICAL EMPLOYMENT

■ 194. ALLOTMENT AND CONTROL.—a. Tank destroyer groups are usually allotted to army corps and field armies as indicated in paragraph 36.

b. In most instances groups will operate under an army corps. They may be attached to divisions when the armored engagement is taking place entirely in a divisional zone or sector, or when the division has an independent or semi-independent mission.

c. The army commander usually will attach the groups assigned to him to the army corps as the situation develops. However, groups operating in an area not occupied by a corps, such as an area to a flank or deep in the army area, usually will remain under control of the army commander.

■ 195. GENERAL.—Tank destroyer groups are intended for action against massed tank forces. As part of the mobile reserve of the high command, they are initially so disposed as to facilitate their rapid entry into action against large armored forces.

a. Tank destroyer groups which are attached to units engaged in offensive combat assist the attack by furnishing protection against large scale counterattacks by hostile tanks. They follow the attack closely, moving by bounds from one position in readiness to another. In enveloping attacks, they are usually echeloned toward the interior behind the enveloping flank.

b. Tank destroyer groups attached to units whose action is defensive are usually held in mobile reserve until the enemy's main effort is indicated and then engaged in mass against the hostile armored force. Depending on the situation, this may be prior to or after the launching of the hostile armored attack.

c. With a view to disrupting the enemy's plans and dispositions and seizing the initiative from his armored forces, tank destroyer groups may be directed, under favorable circumstances, to attack hostile tank concentrations before they have completed their preparations for battle. The support of artillery and combat aviation and the assistance of infantry and tanks will usually be required to break through the enemy's protective screen and allow tank destroyers to assail their objective. The higher commander directing the action may constitute a task force for this purpose.

d. More often, lack of the necessary means of action or of the necessary information will lead the defending commander to hold the tank destroyer group for employment as a counterattacking element. Tanks which have effected, or partially effected, a break-through constitute an ideal objective for tank destroyer groups, since the tanks will frequently have outstripped their accompanying infantry and supporting weapons.

■ 196. OCCUPATION OF PARK.—*a.* The park of the tank destroyer group must be located so as to facilitate expeditious movements to any part of the zone of action of supported troops; usually it will be in the general vicinity of important road crossings. The high degree of mobility of tank destroyer units permits the establishment of bivouacs well to the rear, providing that access to forward areas is not impeded by con-

gested highways or other obstructions, such as defiles, etc.
Hostile aircraft, operating in conjunction with tank forces,
are likely to make tank destroyer groups a primary objective;
parks usually, therefore, will be selected more with regard to
protection from air attack than from ground attack.

b. The group commander insures that the tank destroyer
force is effectively tied into the warning net of supported
troops and that destroyer units are disposed so that they can
move out of bivouac to a zone of action in the shortest possible time. The group will normally be located in an area
approximately 5 miles square or smaller. Subordinate elements are located so as to get the best cover and at the same
time be conveniently located with respect to routes on which
movement is most probable. Separation of subordinate elements by more than 1 or 2 miles is undesirable and usually
unnecessary. Arrangement of subordinate elements is such
as to facilitate contemplated employment. Main roads leading into the area from all directions are covered by security
detachments posted 2 or 3 miles from the group's bivouac.

c. The group commander prescribes the degree of readiness
for action to be maintained; this is progressively increased
with the prospect of early engagement.

d. The group commander causes routes and probable areas
of employment to be reconnoitered by officers. In some cases
plans of action, including order of march and areas of deployment, are prepared. Reconnaissance is also executed to
carry out intelligence missions assigned by higher authority
or to obtain information required by the group. The group
commander employs for this purpose group headquarters
company personnel or mechanized cavalry, when available;
if these do not suffice, he allots missions among tank destroyer battalions which utilize elements of their reconnaissance companies for this purpose.

e. The group commander insures that all available information of the situation is transmitted to his subordinate
units.

■ 197. MARCH.—a. Tank destroyers require priority on roads
when moving to combat. The group commander must insure
that the way will be clear for tank destroyers when need for
their intervention arises. Close coordination of tank de-

stroyer group units with the movement of supported troops is essential.

b. The group commander prescribes the route, march formation, rate of march, and distance between vehicles; these depend on the situation. The proximity of the enemy is the factor which exercises the greatest influence upon march dispositions; these likewise are affected by the probability of hostile air attack and the protection afforded by covering troops. The probability of attack by hostile combat aviation increases with proximity to the enemy, visibility, duration of the movement, the size and compactness of the group, and the utilization of main roads. Observation of a movement by hostile observation aviation usually precedes an attack. Routes will be observed particularly closely when strong forces are approaching one another. Danger is greatest when the situation requires the group to make a daylight march of considerable duration along well-defined roads to meet a hostile armored force. The latter almost invariably will be supported by strong forces of combat aviation. Movements in rear areas which can be completed in less than 3 hours have excellent chances of escaping attack. Small portions of the group effecting isolated movements at night in the rear area will seldom be molested. Columns moving with variable and extended distances between vehicles (5 to 10 to the mile) and at the highest practicable speed are relatively difficult to detect by hostile observation aviation and will not provide profitable targets to combat aviation. Necessary daylight movements are preferably made in this manner if the situation permits; the necessity, however, of passing a large number of troops over a road in a short period of time will often preclude use of such methods by the group.

c. The tank destroyer group preferably moves in more than one column. The number of columns will depend upon the situation and the road net. Formation on the march must correspond to contemplated combat dispositions. When available, mechanized cavalry, motorized infantry, and tanks will usually constitute the leading elements, with destroyer battalions following as a second echelon. One destroyer battalion, earmarked as a reserve, will usually move with rear elements of the group.

d. The group commander provides for the necessary reconnaissance; this is similar in principle to that indicated for the movement of a destroyer battalion. The group employs attached observation aviation and mechanized cavalry to obtain required information or distributes reconnaissance missions among destroyer battalions. Excessive dissipation of reconnaissance elements of tank destroyer battalions should be avoided; necessary employment is characterized by assignment of the major portion of reconnaissance missions to the battalion selected to act initially as group reserve.

e. The group commander prescribes a march objective and may indicate where and when attack orders will be issued. Usually, battalion march objectives are suitable assembly areas; they are assigned with regard to subsequent contemplated employment of battalions (combat echelon or reserve).

f. During the march the group commander is kept informed as to its progress, traffic conditions, and hostile activities by reports from the aviation and ground reconnaissance agencies and by messages from subordinate commanders. He regulates the movement accordingly, prescribing new routes or march objectives when required by the situation.

■ 198. ENTRY INTO ACTION.—*a.* Whenever practicable, the group organizes its combat action while subordinate elements are occupying their assembly areas. Measures may be limited to announcement of the situation, the contemplated plan of action, and instructions to leading elements for reconnaissance and covering of a further advance.

b. The group commander, in accordance with his estimates of the situation, determines appropriate missions for the various components of the group. In particular he decides whether tank destroyer battalions are to constitute the combat echelon initially or whether preliminary action by other elements is required. The group commander insures the proper coordination of the action of his own forces and that of other friendly troops in the vicinity.

c. Orders are based upon data which include information of the enemy, instructions from higher authority, the situation and contemplated action of adjacent units, fire support, and the terrain.

■ 199. PLAN OF ACTION.—*a.* The plan of action of the group commander usually provides for blocking or engaging the

118

enemy frontally in conjunction with a blow at his flanks or rear. As soon as possible the group endeavors to gain control of routes over which the enemy has advanced.

b. Utilizing its ground and air reconnaissance, the group usually advances on a broad front with two tank destroyer battalions abreast and one in reserve. Only one tank destroyer battalion may be used in the combat echelon in vague situations; initial engagement of all tank destroyer battalions will usually be limited to situations in which both flanks of the group are protected by other troops or the situation is such that the full strength of the group must be exerted at once.

c. Tanks and infantry, depending on the situation, precede the tank destroyer battalions or are held in reserve. Mechanized cavalry elements continue their reconnaissance missions and cover the flanks. After the combat echelon has become engaged, the reserve may be maneuvered to assist in the action against the hostile flanks and rear, used to support elements engaged frontally, or continued in reserve until suitable opportunity arises for its employment.

d. When hostile tanks are preceded or covered by foot troops, the group commander decides whether to engage the latter with his attached infantry or to effect a rapid penetration with attached tanks followed by destroyers. Attacking infantry may be supported by direct fire of destroyers using high explosive shell.

■ 200. CONDUCT OF ACTION.—The group commander conducts the action from a location where he can best control his battalions, receive information, and wherever practicable personally observe the action. He engages his reserve in accordance with the situation, alters previously assigned missions of subordinate units, or assigns entirely new missions in accordance with developments. By means of his ground and air reconnaissance and reports of engaged units, he keeps informed concerning the situation, and maneuvers his battalions so as to have superior forces in the selected area of contact. He endeavors to hem the enemy into restricted areas facilitating his destruction. He reconstitutes a reserve at the earliest opportunity after engaging his original reserve. In so doing, he respects the integrity of tactical units so far as is practicable. Control of subordinate elements in combat is normally by voice radio.

■ 201. REORGANIZATION.—The group commander indicates the time and general area for reorganization and the time at which subordinate elements should be ready for further combat employment. He may indicate a location at which commanders report for further orders.

■ 202. WITHDRAWAL.—The group commander assigns routes to subordinate units and indicates the time at which withdrawal is to begin and the ultimate or initial destination, together with contemplated dispositions there. He may detail a covering force. Separate routes are assigned to each battalion whenever practicable.

■ 203. PURSUIT.—The group usually pursues on a wide front combining direct pressure and encirclement. The group commander assigns missions to battalions, a portion of which are directed so as to intercept the retreating enemy. Decentralization of control is usual.

SECTION III

GROUP HEADQUARTERS AND HEADQUARTERS
COMPANY

■ 204. COMPOSITION AND MISSION.—a. Group headquarters and headquarters company is organized as indicated in T/O 18–10–1.

b. The principal mission of headquarters company is to furnish the necessary enlisted assistants for the group commander and his staff and to provide for their immediate security. When the latter mission is unnecessary, security elements of headquarters company may be used for reconnaissance.

c. The various elements of headquarters company perform their functions at or in the vicinity of the group command post or, in case the group includes attached service elements, at the park. (See FM 18–10.)

■ 205. COMMAND POST.—a. In park.—In a park or intermediate position the group command post is usually centrally located with respect to subordinate elements. Provision is made to allow approximately a dozen officers and enlisted men to work in the command post by night under adequate lighting, or to assemble officers conveniently by night, for conferences or to receive orders or information.

b. *On the march.*—On the march the command post usually moves behind the bulk of the combat elements. The command post is advanced to a new location in preparation for combat when its previous location is too far from the area of probable action for effective communication with subordinate units. Movement in such case is usually effected by bounds; a forward echelon is sent forward as early as the situation permits; when it has been established, the remainder of the command post advances. A bound of less than 10 to 15 miles is seldom justified.

c. *In combat.*—(1) The command post is organized so that the commander, with a party containing adequate means of communication, can go where his presence is necessary best to control the action, while the bulk of the command post continues to function from a stationary location, facilitating communication with higher authority, aviation, and supply services.

(2) The commander's party normally includes S–2 and S–3; it consists of armored vehicles providing radio communication with the command post and with principal subordinate units. The party is protected by a portion of the security section of group headquarters company. Liaison officers of major subordinate elements accompany the commander.

(3) The executive remains at the command post during combat. He supervises administrative arrangements, keeps informed as to the situation, and is prepared to take over promptly in case the commander becomes a casualty. He insures the prompt relaying to the commander of important orders and information.

■ 206. LIAISON OFFICERS.—The group maintains liaison officers at the command post of the large unit to which it is allocated, and may send representatives to other units with which it is likely to operate. The liaison officers keep the group informed as to the general situation and plans for employment of the group. Periodical summaries are transmitted by messenger or personal contact, important changes being sent by radio.

■ 207. LIAISON WITH SUPPORT AVIATION.—*a*. The group headquarters maintains close liaison with combat support aviation designated to cooperate with it. Plans and arrangements for missions are effected in advance by conferences. Air forces personnel are provided with maps marked in the coordinate code that is in use in the group. These preliminary conferences insure prompt arrival of combat aviation when need arises, and reach agreement upon methods of target designation and communication. Whenever practicable, support aviation personnel, which is actually to execute tasks in support of tank destroyer units, should participate in the conferences. Information concerning agreements reached should be thoroughly disseminated to subordinate tank destroyer units. Positive means of identifying tank destroyer units and vehicles to support aviation must be provided and must be understood by the appropriate ground and air units.

b. Tank destroyer units must realize that small targets, due to dispersion, camouflage, or concealment, are not suitable targets for support aviation.

c. It is essential that tank destroyers indicate to aircraft the location of targets on the ground. Reliance on map coordinates or descriptions alone will not suffice. The following methods may be used:

(1) Firing of specified pyrotechnics by tank destroyers posted in front and on the flanks of the target areas.

(2) Pointing with panels, with range indicated by a proper number of cross bars or discs, each representing a definite distance.

(3) Vehicles in prearranged formation.

(4) Smoke to mark a reference point.

(5) Signal lamps and lights.

d. When practicable, tank destroyer unit observers are posted to note effectiveness of bombing attack and report by radio errors in selection of targets.

e. For details concerning the action of aviation in support of ground forces, see FM 31–35.

CHAPTER 10

DISMOUNTED TANK HUNTING

■ 208. GENERAL.—While tank destroyer units' principal method of action against tanks is fire and movement by antitank cannon, many occasions will occur where dismounted tank hunting methods may be effectively employed by tank destroyer personnel. Any type of tank may be destroyed by close combat weapons in the hands of courageous, aggressive men. Such action by individuals or small parties is inherent in tank destroyer combat. When their main weapons have been knocked out, all tank destroyer crews continue to fight hostile tanks effectively. Small units may be used to attack tanks in a park or bivouac. Reconnaissance and security elements will frequently be offered the opportunity to attack tanks which attempt flanking action through woods.

■ 209. EMPLOYMENT OF CLOSE COMBAT WEAPONS.—*a.* The antitank grenade is the principal weapon used by tank hunters. It is preferably employed against known weak spots in armor.

b. Accurate small arms fire at close range will reduce the fighting efficiency of the tank. Targets are: exposed crew members; periscopes (fire will not break the glass, but will shatter the lens, making vision impossible); slits (they are usually too small to permit the passage of a small arms projectile; however, lead spray will cause the crew to close slits or suffer casualties); turret rings (a direct hit on the turret ring will seal the turret and tank hull, preventing rotation); driving sprockets (direct hits in the driving sprockets may reduce tank mobility); radio aerial and aerial base (this will not necessarily prevent communication, but will cause radio interference). Tank hunters use small arms fire to kill crews of tanks disabled by antitank mines.

c. Incendiary grenades are employed against horizontal surfaces of tanks or crevices where inflammable substances will collect. Coatings of grease and oil which gather on the surface, ventilation ports which draw flame into tanks, or burning of the motor when flame filters through engine coverings render all tanks vulnerable to flames.

123

d. Antitank mines are used mainly against the running gear of tanks. Once stopped, tanks are destroyed with incendiary or antitank grenades. Large mines or two or three 10-pound mines placed together will stave in the belly of the tank, killing the crew. Mines are employed in ambushes to block and destroy leading and rearmost tanks, or to deny ground to tanks.

e. Antitank bombs, improvised from 10 pounds of TNT or nitrostarch, are most effective when placed in tracks and detonated, or dropped on the top of tanks where armor is thin. The explosion usually staves in the top armor or engine covering.

f. Smoke is used to blind the tank and confuse the crew; it enables tank hunters to work close to the tank unobserved. Smoke also may be used to isolate tanks so that mutual support is impossible. Smoke may be laid by smoke pot or FM grenade. White phosphorus grenades also are good smoke-producing weapons.

g. The use of all close combat weapons against tanks is such as to capitalize on the limitations on the free use of tank weapons. Although some tank weapons have all-around traverse, visibility of gunners is limited to narrow lanes. Tank weapons are limited in depression, causing a dead space near the tank ranging from 20 to sometimes 30 feet. Turrets require up to 15 seconds to traverse the full 360°.

■ 210. ORGANIZATION OF TANK HUNTING PARTIES.—Tank hunting organization is dictated by the terrain and situation. As a rule, small parties are most effective. Where many men are available and needed, several parties operate on the same mission with close cooperation. Tank hunting operations are of three distinct types, each type requiring different methods.

a. Emergency action.—Tank hunters, keeping well concealed, work in small groups, deployed in depth along probable routes of advance of hostile armored units. From slit trenches or other concealed and protected areas, tank hunters assail tanks, using the type "A" grenade (rifle or hand), incendiary grenades, and small arms fire. They withhold fire until tanks can be assailed from several sides; this may require that reconnaissance and leading elements of enemy armored units be permitted to bypass the foremost tank hunter groups. Tank hunter groups may be used to deny wooded or covered areas to enemy tanks and force the latter into regions where primary tank destroyer weapons have good fields of fire.

b. Ambush.—In the ambush surprise is essential. Wits should be used rather than rules. The obvious should be avoided and the enemy should be misled and mystified. Variations in ambushes are unlimited. In all phases of ambush, concealment is the primary consideration. Varying factors are the terrain, the formation and strength of enemy, the strength of our own forces, and available weapons.

(1) The following general guides are suggested:

(*a*) Through reconnaissance select a suitable site.

(*b*) Endeavor to locate defiles (a road flanked by high banks or woods, villages, towns, etc.).

(*c*) Avoid places that are too obvious, especially when an easy detour is available for a suspicious enemy.

(2) A definite plan should be made for each ambush, and must be thoroughly understood by all tank hunters. In general the following should be included:

(*a*) At each end of the ambush, place observation posts (scouts).

(*b*) If time permits, dig slit trenches.

(*c*) Provide foolproof signals for the announcement of enemy approach (visual or sound).

(*d*) Devise methods to stop reconnaissance units *after they have passed* the ambush site (wire, ropes, etc., stretched diagonally across road as motorcyclist arrives at proper point.

(*e*) Devise method of stopping the first tank so that remaining tanks will then stop or crash into it (barricades, trees felled by explosives at proper instant, AT mines, AT guns, etc.).

(*f*) Provide means of preventing escape, that is, mines across roads or road block.

(*g*) With smoke or explosives, isolate tanks so that mutual tank support is impossible.

(*h*) Designate a tank hunting team to destroy each tank anticipated; 3 men on first tank, 3 men on second, etc.

(*i*) Provide flank observation for protection.

(*j*) Stress concealment of men and equipment, weapons and vehicles; otherwise surprise is sacrificed.

(*k*) Visualize sequence of events, and inform all individuals.

(*l*) Rehearse ambush if time permits.

(*m*) Check weapons and sector of fire.

(*n*) Arrange and reconnoiter routes of withdrawal to rallying positions.

(o) Give detailed information as to how to deal with tank crews which may be capable of dismounted action.

(3) Trained personnel should be employed. They must be highly disciplined and capable of holding fire until the exact moment required.

c. Raids.—Prior to a raid, tank hunters locate tank parts by reconnaissance. Tank hunters then raid the harbored tanks, killing the crews and destroying armored vehicles by flame and explosives. Raids must be carefully planned. Raiding parties must be small. When large numbers of raiders are required, several parties may operate in conjunction. Information obtained by previous reconnaissance should give the exact location of enemy tanks, nature of terrain, number and location of sentinels, outguards, etc. The size and perimeter of a park and the approximate number of tanks contained therein should be know definitely, as well as routes of approach and retreat. Success of tank hunter raids depends on surprise. The tank hunters strike silently and quickly, cause as much damage as possible, and rally outside the tank park. In terrain offering little or no concealment, one group may be employed to illuminate one side of the park with flares and other pyrotechnics while a second group fires upon the enemy silhouetted against the light. Care is taken to prevent exposure of the first group to the fire of the second. Personnel for raids should be carefully selected.

CHAPTER 11

ANTITANK WARNING SERVICE

■ **211. How Prescribed.**—The general organization of the antitank warning service and the methods to be employed are prescribed by higher commanders. Usually this will include the method of reporting information, assignment of zones of responsibility for reconnaissance and observation to subordinate elements, and instructions concerning the prompt transmission of information.

■ **212. Sources of Information.**—Reconnaissance and observation agencies, particularly aviation, are very important sources of information, but every unit forms part of the warning service. It may be likened to a fire alarm system in a city, with every citizen a potential giver of the alarm.

■ **213. Form of Messages.**—A uniform type of tank warning message is usually prescribed to expedite and simplify transmission of information. Such a message usually includes in a predetermined sequence the number of tanks seen, their type, location, direction of movement, and the time at which they were seen. One type of map only is used in reporting tank warnings.

■ **214. Warning Nets.**—*a.* Arrangement of warning nets varies; the following system appears generally applicable. Certain radio stations in each division and attached units remain constantly open on a prescribed frequency. Only tank warning information is sent over the net. The number of sets in the net is limited; one per battalion or regiment is usual. Any information obtained is flashed over this net. The station at division headquarters is located in a focal center which operates under the division antitank officer. The focal center has a plotting board. It receives all tank flashes, analyzes and interprets the information, and plots hostile movements. The information is conveyed to the designated division staff officer and also flashed over another radio to the tank warning net of corps and army.

b. Within the smaller units tank warnings move through command communication channels but are given priority.

c. A corps and army warning net operates in a similar manner. Stations in the net include each division, corps, and army focal center. Corps and army reconnaissance agencies operate in a separate corps or army net similar to the divisional net. Their information is relayed in a similar manner.

d. Interlocking of nets through the focal centers insures that information will be analyzed before being transmitted, without materially retarding transmission.

■ **215.** TANK DESTROYER UNITS.—*a.* Tank destroyer battalions and groups will have radio sets in the warning nets of the units to which allocated.

b. For their security they provide a local warning service of their own. They may be charged with reconnaissance and observation over a prescribed area. The information gained by reconnaissance is flashed to battalion headquarters, where it is transmitted over the radio on the warning net.

CHAPTER 12

TRAINING

SECTION I

TRAINING OBJECTIVES

■ 216.—GENERAL.—*a.* The ultimate of all military training is victory in battle. The conditions facing an army in war cannot always be definitely foreseen. It must be trained to function effectively in any climate or terrain. The fundamental training doctrines are prescribed in FM 100–5, FM 21–5, and in this manual.

b. Training will be so conducted as to develop the ability and desire to take offensive action in combat. Detailed instructions are contained in field manuals and technical manuals, in mobilization regulations, and in training circulars and directives.

c. To develop the offensive spirit, a major objective of training must be the development of aggressive individuals and units whose skill with weapons have instilled in them confidence in their ability to destroy the enemy both at long range and in close combat.

d. Successful offensive action demands that military training develop in the individual and in the unit the following qualities:

> Morale.
> Discipline.
> Health, strength, and endurance.
> Technical proficiency.
> Initiative.
> Adaptability.
> Leadership.
> Teamwork.
> Tactical proficiency.

e. The commander of an organization must analyze carefully the training mission or objective designated by a higher echelon to ascertain precisely what he is expected to accomplish. Each commander must analyze his own requirements and assure himself that the training objective he has designated can be attained. if the time, facilities, and personnel are properly employed.

■ 217. TRAINING THE INDIVIDUAL.—*a.* The object of individual training is the development of the skill and knowledge necessary to enable the individual to play his part effectively in the fighting team in order that he can kill, or help kill, his enemy before his enemy can kill him or his comrades.

b. Every opportunity during training will be utilized to create enthusiasm and interest, to stimulate alertness, pride in personal appearance, sense of responsibility, and to develop initiative and esprit de corps. (See FM 21–5.)

■ 218. TRAINING IN LEADERSHIP.—The qualities of leadership must be developed to a high degree in all grades. The ability to analyze situations basically and quickly, to reach sound decisions, and to give expression thereto in concise and clear orders will be developed in all leaders through frequent tactical exercises.

■ 219. UNIT TRAINING.—The training objective of the tank destroyer unit is to produce a team composed of individuals, squads, sections, platoons, and companies each with a high degree of individual and group skill which will apply on the battlefield the proper tank destroyer technique and tactical doctrine.

SECTION II

INDIVIDUAL TRAINING

■ 220. SCOPE.—The purpose of this section is to explain the adaptation of certain subjects covered in pertinent field manuals on training to tank destroyer training and to furnish additional training suggestions.

■ 221. VERSATILITY.—Throughout tank destroyer units, it is essential that officers and enlisted men be thoroughly trained in their regularly assigned duties, and in addition, they must become proficient in other assignments. This requirement is necessary so that fighting efficiency will be maintained in spite of casualties. Training of the individual in multiple assignments is subordinated to training in his primary assignment until he has become reasonably proficient.

■ 222. INDIVIDUAL TRAINING.—*a.* Members of tank destroyer squads will be trained in antiaircraft gun marksmanship; members of the antiaircraft squad, likewise, will be trained in the tank destroyer squads' individual duties and in tank destroyer gun marksmanship.

b. Members of the security section will be trained as replacements for both tank destroyer and antiaircraft squads. Replacement training will include firing weapons.

c. Reconnaissance platoons will be trained in pioneer operations; members of pioneer platoons will be trained in accordance with FM 21-45.

d. Each individual will be highly trained in marksmanship with his individual weapon and with those weapons assigned to his section.

e. The general objective in driver training should be: all drivers and all officers able to drive any vehicle in the unit. Specifically, all personnel assigned to a vehicle should be able to drive it; company commanders will train at least two fully competent replacement drivers for each vehicle. (See FM 25-10.)

f. All personnel will be trained in weapon, tank, and other vehicle destruction employing individual, section, and improvised weapons, and in tank hunting. (See ch. 10.)

g. All personnel will be trained in the employment of motor vehicle field expedients. (See FM 25-10.)

h. Training films and film strips are exceedingly valuable training aids which have particular application in the training of the individual. For list of current training films and methods of use, see FM 21-6.

■ 223. PHYSICAL TRAINING.—*a. General.*—The tactical employment of tank destroyer units will place a heavy drain on the physical stamina of the individual; therefore, special attention must be given physical conditioning. (See FM 21-20.)

b. Calisthenics.—A comparatively small amount of time

allotted to physical training will be devoted to formal calisthenics.

c. *Marching.*—Long marches, combined with hard physical labor, probably is the best method of toughening; but this method requires much time and does not teach coordination.

d. *Athletics.*—Contests, both mass and personal, never fail to produce rivalry for superiority and at the same time develop mental and physical alertness, coordination, and unit or group spirit, and give variety and interest to the physical training program.

e. *Athletic facilities.*—Company commanders should procure, install, and maintain in good condition as much athletic equipment as funds and issued articles will provide.

f. *Injuries.*—Some injuries may result from strenuous games and exercise, but must be kept to the minimum by the use of exercises of progressive intensity. However, the strenuous program of development and conditioning will not be abandoned because of injuries to a few men. Men with minor injuries should be excused only from those exercises that might aggravate their injury.

■ 224. DISCIPLINARY TRAINING.—In addition to other drills, short recurrent periods devoted to service of the piece and gun drills, and executed with meticulous precision, constitute valuable training.

■ 225. MARKSMANSHIP.—a. Details of marksmanship training are covered in Field Manuals and in Technical Manuals pertaining to each weapon.

b. Training in marksmanship for tank destroyer units must be thorough and continuous; organizations that cannot shoot will not live on the battlefield. Tank destroyer action is rapid and the effect of both tank destroyer and tank fire is extremely destructive. Gunners must therefore develop speed and accuracy of marksmanship well above formerly accepted standards.

c. Thorough preliminary training, use of training expedients, and subcaliber and field firing will be utilized. After proficiency has been gained, troops must continue marksmanship practice to obviate loss of skill from lack of practice.

d. (1) Gunners should be instructed in the elements of

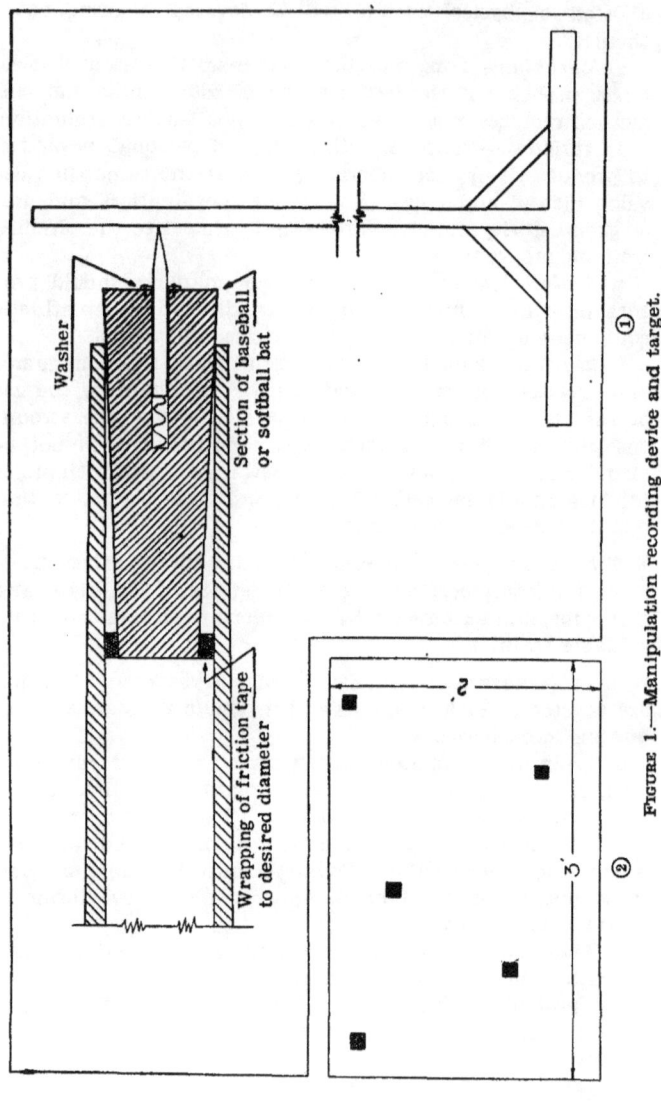

FIGURE 1.—Manipulation recording device and target.

ballistics and effect of fire. Their ability to estimate ranges under combat conditions must be developed.

(2) Gunners should be taught the theory of leads and afforded frequent opportunity for practice. The ability to estimate leads rapidly and accurately is of great importance and requires practice.

e. Training expedients will be utilized to the full extent of facilities and ingenuity. Expedients add interest to preliminary practice and show the results of instruction to both the student and the instructor. Numerous expedients are described in FM 21–5. Another device for teaching coordination and recording ability to coordinate is illustrated in figure 1①. A tapered cylindrical plug that contains a pencil size recess with a light coiled spring at its base is inserted in the muzzle of the gun. A stand is placed in front of the muzzle for recording on paper the result of the tracking. A target, approximate size 2 feet by 3 feet, is placed about 1,000 inches away (see fig. 1②). The student tracks from spotter to spotter, forming an irregular W. His first efforts probably will result in a series of irregular steps, but practice will quickly teach the student how to manipulate his piece so that the resultant tracking is a straight, or nearly straight, line.

f. Subcalibers may be improvised by mounting a caliber .22 or .30 rifle in or upon the tube of 37-mm or larger guns. Subcaliber firing should be as realistic as local conditions permit. Caliber .22 firing is effective in training as far as the dust raised by the bullet's impact can be seen; training in firing caliber .30 tracer ammunition is most effective at ranges up to 500 yards; beyond this range the sights are not accurate due to the difference between the trajectories of subcaliber and service ammunition. Realism is added by the use of ingenuity in the adaptation of moving targets to the types of ranges available.

g. Field firing with practice ammunition should not consist of firing from a prepared position only; crews should receive training in combining fire and movement. Target should be both visible and partly concealed; they should appear from unexpected, as well as expected, locations.

■ 226. DRIVING.—a. Drivers of tank destroyer vehicles must be trained beyond ordinary standards. Further details will be found in FM 25–10 and FM 18–15. Emphasis will be placed upon cross country and other forms of difficult driving. Cross country instruction should not be confined to driving courses, but should include driving over rough, untraveled terrain and the type of ground that will be encountered in combat. Only experience will teach the capabilities and limitations of vehicles.

b. Instruction in night driving without lights, on roads and cross country, will be stressed. The instruction should include teamwork between the driver and assistant driver, noncommissioned officer, or officer who rides beside him. Instruction in night driving should start with easy exercises and progress from driving with a bright moon to darker conditions in bad weather. The route should be easy at first. After proficiency is gained under good conditions, exercises of gradually increasing difficulty are executed.

c. Desert driving calls for the highest skill on the part of the driver, since the necessity of dispersion and of avoiding sharp turns and the tracks of a preceding vehicle will require a high degree of individual effort. The driver must be taught the proper use of gears in sand driving, and the use of expedients for extricating equipment once it is stuck in the sand. Details are included in FM 31–25.

■ 227. MAINTENANCE AND SALVAGE.—a. General.—Details pertinent to maintenance and salvage will be found in technical manuals on each type of matériel and FM 25–10.

b. Preventive maintenance.—The tremendous importance of preventive maintenance of motor vehicles will be emphasized. This consists of recognizing minor defects before they result in major breakdowns. (See FM 18–15.)

c. Reports of damage and malfunctioning.—All personnel must be imbued with the requirement of instantly reporting any damage to, or malfunctioning of, any piece of matériel that comes to their attention. All personnel will continuously inspect all matériel assigned to them for service ability and cleanliness. Drivers will inspect their vehicles at every halt.

d. Weapon maintenance and salvage.—(1) All gun crews will be instructed in the care, operation, and field repair of weapons. The crew should be able to perform most repair work, except that involving the recoil mechanism, and in combat emergencies be able to salvage damaged weapons and build serviceable weapons by combining parts from two or more guns.

(2) Motor vehicle recovery and salvage in combat will require the utmost in resourcefulness and ingenuity. Salvage operations should be practiced during field exercises.

■ 228. IDENTIFICATION OF AIRCRAFT AND ARMORED AND UNARMORED VEHICLES.—Instruction in prompt identification is continuous. Full use is made of charts, which of necessity may be improvised under field conditions, and of field manuals of the 30 series covering identification of U. S. and foreign vehicles and aircraft. Recent battle experience has clearly demonstrated the critical importance of recognition of *friendly* matériel. Charts should be displayed in mess halls, recreation rooms, squad rooms, or on bulletin boards. Captured vehicles should be used in the instruction when possible. The latest information of enemy matériel should be passed down to all personnel. In addition to being taught· identification by sight and sound, personnel should be instructed in possible identification by action; this is particularly important in teaching the identification of leaders' tanks. Personnel, especially reconnaissance elements, should learn to identify by tire imprints what vehicle has passed. Troops will be warned about the possibility of the enemy using captured vehicles;.this warning will be emphasized when operations are within a theater in which it is known or believed that the enemy has captured armored vehicles from our own or allied forces.

■ 229. TERRAIN APPRECIATION.—*a.* Terrain appreciation is the ability to observe and interpret accurately all important terrain characteristics from ground, aerial, or map reconnaissance in order to provide for the correct tactical use of the ground and complete employment of available natural cover. This ability can be acquired only through extensive training and field reconnaissance experience. Training in this phase of reconnaissance should emphasize, and develop proficiency in, observing and recognizing the following:

(1) Terrain features, areas, and objects to be avoided, including those—

(*a*) Lacking sufficient natural cover.

(b) Not readily passable by the type vehicles in use.

(c) Open to direct observation regardless of overhead cover, ridges, and crests.

(d) Unusually prominent and logical registration points for enemy artillery and bombing.

(2) Routes of approach or attack, or areas to be occupied which offer best natural cover (overhead and defilade).

(3) Particular types of terrain which permit the utilization of the superior mobility of our own vehicles over enemy tanks.

b. It is essential to train and perfect in terrain appreciation leaders of all units from the section to the battalion. Training of units of any size to employ correct use of ground and cover is a part of tactical training and of protective measures. (See also FM 101-5.)

■ 230. RECONNAISSANCE AND SECURITY.—*a. Reconnaissance.*— The elementary phases of reconnaissance may be taught with blackboards, maps, or sand tables, or by combination of these. Numerous practical exercises in mounted and dismounted scouting and selection of routes are required *to* develop reasonable proficiency in reconnaissance.

b. Security.—The instructor emphasizes the constant need for security measures. (See FM 21-100 and FM 21-45.) Elementary lessons given indoors should be followed by practical work; advanced training is conducted in connection with field exercises. All commanders continuously inspect security measures, making corrections and giving constructive criticisms when necessary.

■ 231. SIGNAL COMMUNICATION.—*a.* Tank destroyer communication training will cover radio, messengers, panels, pyrotechnics, smoke, flag, and improvised blinker signals, as outlined in FM 24-5.

(1) The technical training of radio operators is amply covered in FM 24 series, and in TM 11-454. Radio operators are permanently assigned to the same set and to the same station in the net. Efficient teamwork between the radio operator and his commander requires familiarity and constant work together.

(2) Communication personnel should be trained in the use of auxiliary and improvised methods of signal communication after they have become proficient in the normal

methods. Radio operators must also be capable of acting as drivers and gunners.

b. Codes and ciphers used are the air-ground liaison, division field, geographical codes, and the cipher device M–94 and converter MC–209.

(1) Training methods for the various issued codes and ciphers are described in current publications.

(2) Since tank destroyer units frequently will operate under different headquarters, each headquarters possibly using different geographic codes, tank destroyer communication and staff personnel will be trained in the various devices. Some of these devices are—

(*a*) Templates of various types which are placed on a map in a secretly designated manner, locations being referred to by template readings.

(*b*) Geographic codes in which towns and other prominent points are given code names.

(*c*) Coordinate codes secretly designating the normal X and Y coordinates by letters or numerals other than those printed on the map.

(*d*) Polar coordinates by which points are designated by the azimuth and the distance from a secretly designated point. The protractor may be in degrees or mils or it may be a clock face.

(*e*) Offset method in which a secret line is drawn north and south, or several degrees from the north-south line, on a map. Points are designated in inches up from the bottom of the map and right or left from the line. Example: A point 10 inches up the map and 3½ inches to the right of the line is described as 10 R 3.5.

(*f*) Double azimuth method by which a point is designated by the intersection of two azimuths drawn from two different secretly designated points on a map or from two secretly designated terrain features on the ground. This method has the advantage that different scale maps can be used.

c. Signal operation instructions will be simple and conform so far as possible to the form used in FM 24–5.

■ 232. INTELLIGENCE, COUNTERINTELLIGENCE, AND INFORMATION.—*a.* All personnel will be trained in the gathering and reporting of military information. Special emphasis will be placed on prompt reporting of information to intelligence agencies. The intelligence personnel of headquarters company will be thoroughly trained by S-2 in the collection, evaluation, and dissemination of military information.

b. All personnel will be thoroughly trained by conferences, demonstrations, and field exercises in the importance of camouflage and camouflage discipline. Emphasis in training will be placed on the importance of secrecy. All officers and noncommissioned officers will be trained in the employment of all counterintelligence measures. (See FM 30–25 and FM 5–20.)

■ 233. CHEMICALS.—Training should include the frequent wearing of the mask during exercises. Decontamination methods and the use of tactical smoke will be given practical application during field exercises. Tactics and methods of defense against chemicals will be found in FM 21–40 and FM 100–5.

SECTION III

UNIT TRAINING

■ 234. GENERAL.—*a.* Unit training is designed to promote the development of teamwork and leadership, and the application of technique and tactical doctrine to combat situations.

b. The primary training objective of each tank destroyer unit will be the early development of an efficient, hard-striking unit which is prepared to take the field at short notice, at existing strength, and capable of conducting combined operations against an enemy equipped with modern means of warfare.

c. Unit training commences with the thorough training of small units. No matter how well larger unit training is conducted, efficient companies, battalions, and groups cannot be built around a group of stupidly trained squads, sections, and platoons.

■ 235. TEAMWORK.—*a.* Men are grouped into units with a view to their training for and use in combat. The combat group acquires cohesion through common experience. Individuals constantly trained, quartered, and fed together develop a feeling of solidarity, which must be furthered by the greatest degree of permanence being given to squad, section, and platoon assignments. (See FM 100–5 and FM 21–5.)

b. Units will fight in small groups, often removed from the direct influence of officers, and derive their cohesion from the unity inculcated by association and training. Teamwork is based on the belief that the team task can be accomplished, the knowledge that the leadership is competent, and the confidence that each member of the team will perform his share of the task.

■ 236. DISCIPLINE AND MORALE.—*a*. The combat value of a unit is determined in a great measure by the soldierly qualities of its leaders and members and its will to fight. Discipline is the main cohesive force that binds the members of a unit. The leader must set before all a high standard of military conduct and apply to all the same rules of discipline.

b. Individuals of a unit habitually act in accordance with the military standards which the group has accepted. Every effort must be made to develop the pride of individuals in their group. Good morale and a sense of duty in a command cannot be improvised; they must be thoroughly planned and systematically promoted.

c. Every leader must take energetic action against indiscipline, panic, pillage, and other disruptive influences. The morale of a unit is that of its leader.

■ 237. FIGHTING PROFICIENCY.—*a*. Success in battle depends upon the coordinated employment of all available arms and techniques applicable to the situation. This coordination is obtained only through painstaking combined training of highly trained individuals and units. Tactical flexibility is based on the ability to exact definite and rigid standards of performance from individuals committed to action.

b. Training and discipline impart the cohesion and confidence that will prevent faltering and carry a unit through the demoralizing impressions caused by unexpected events in combat.

Appendix I

ILLUSTRATIONS

The illustrations in this appendix should be used as a guide in learning tactical methods; they cannot be followed under many conditions. Methods that are successful in one situation might result in a disastrous failure when applied to a different situation. For instance, a flank attack against an armored force might be very successful; such an attack might fail because of strong hostile flank protection. Methods used should vary; tank destroyer commanders should use every opportunity to deliver the unexpected.

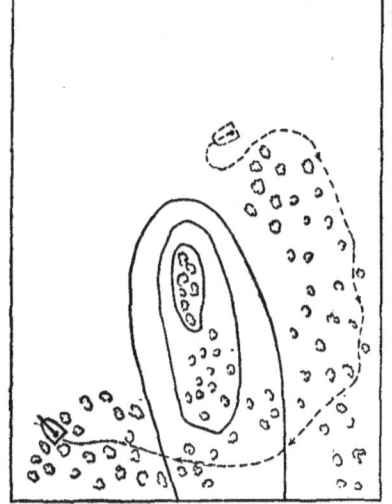

① WRONG. Unnecessary exposure during lateral movement across front.

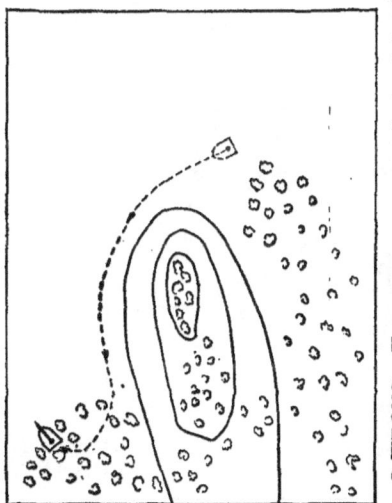

② RIGHT. Proper use of cover and avoidance of exposed lateral movement. Applicable to units of any size.

FIGURE 2.—Movement.

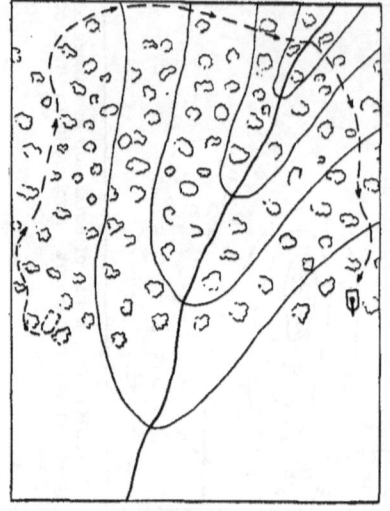

② RIGHT. Prompt movement as the result of prior reconnaissance. Applicable to all units.

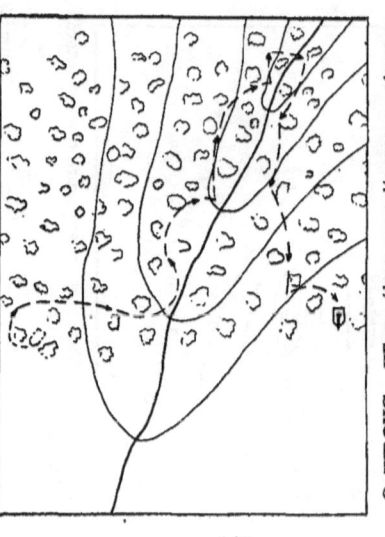

① WRONG. When time permits reconnaissance for alternate and supplementary positions. Failure to reconnoiter causes delay while searching for passable routes.

FIGURE 3.—Movement to alternate or supplementary position.

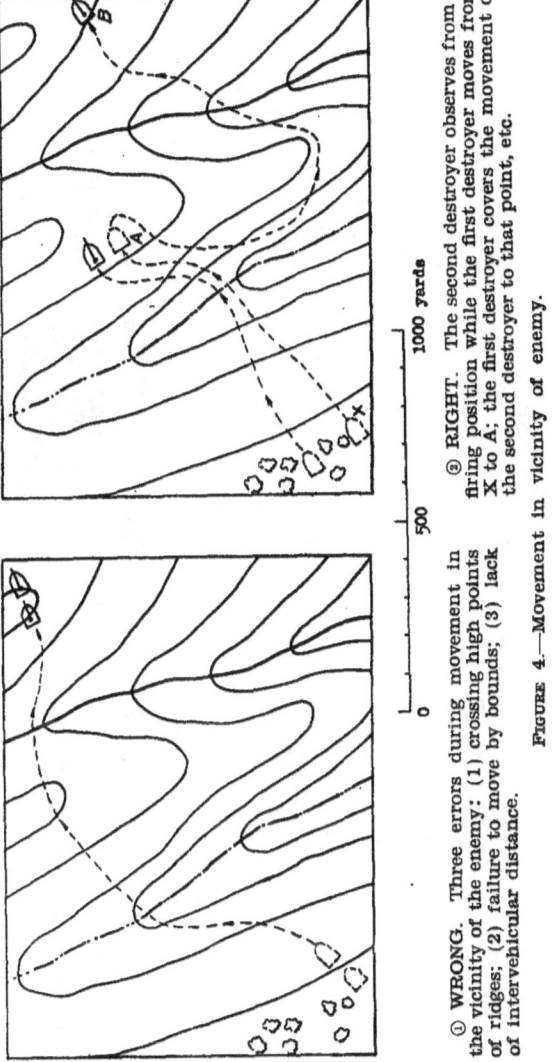

① WRONG. Three errors during movement in the vicinity of the enemy: (1) crossing high points of ridges; (2) failure to move by bounds; (3) lack of intervehicular distance.

② RIGHT. The second destroyer observes from a firing position while the first destroyer moves from X to A; the first destroyer covers the movement of the second destroyer to that point, etc.

FIGURE 4.—Movement in vicinity of enemy.

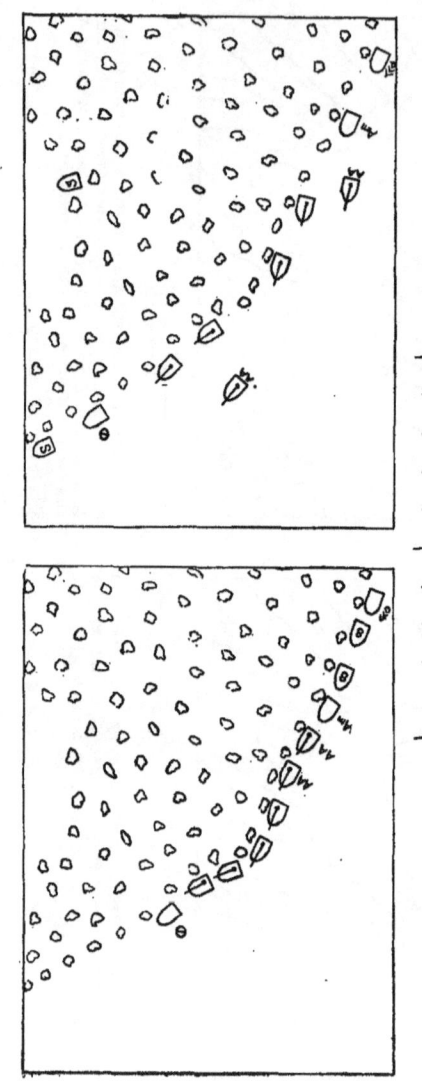

① WRONG. Three errors during an approach march; (1) no security; (2) antiaircraft guns not dispersed along column; (3) insufficient intervehicular distance.

② RIGHT. Security to front and on exposed flank; platoon leader well forward; ample intervehicular distance; antiaircraft guns dispersed along column away from obstructions to aerial fire or, if secrecy is desired, dispersed within the column prepared to rush into the open.

200 yards

100

0

FIGURE 5.—Movement—platoon in approach march.

145

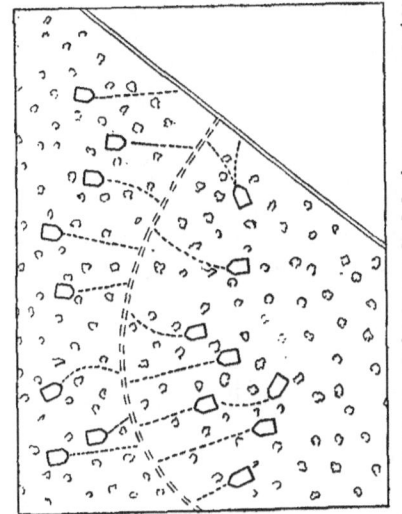
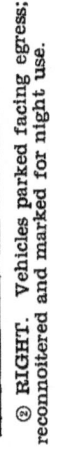

② RIGHT. Vehicles parked facing egress; routes reconnoitered and marked for night use.

FIGURE 6.—Parking (security elements not shown).

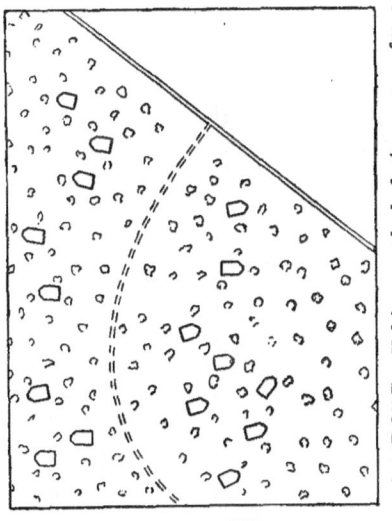

① WRONG. Vehicles parked facing away from routes of egress, which causes an excessive delay when leaving a park, bivouac, assembly position, or position in readiness.

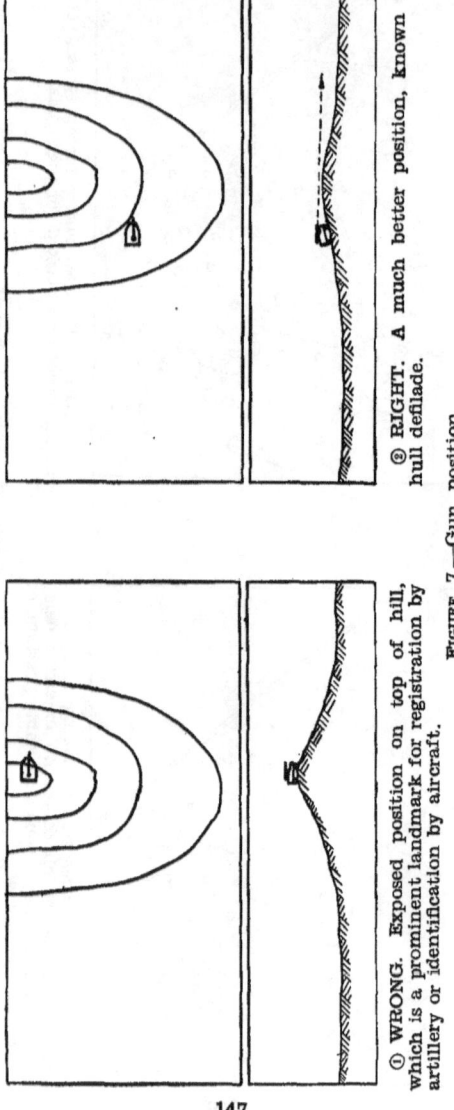

① WRONG. Exposed position on top of hill, which is a prominent landmark for registration by artillery or identification by aircraft.

② RIGHT. A much better position, known as hull defilade.

FIGURE 7.—Gun position.

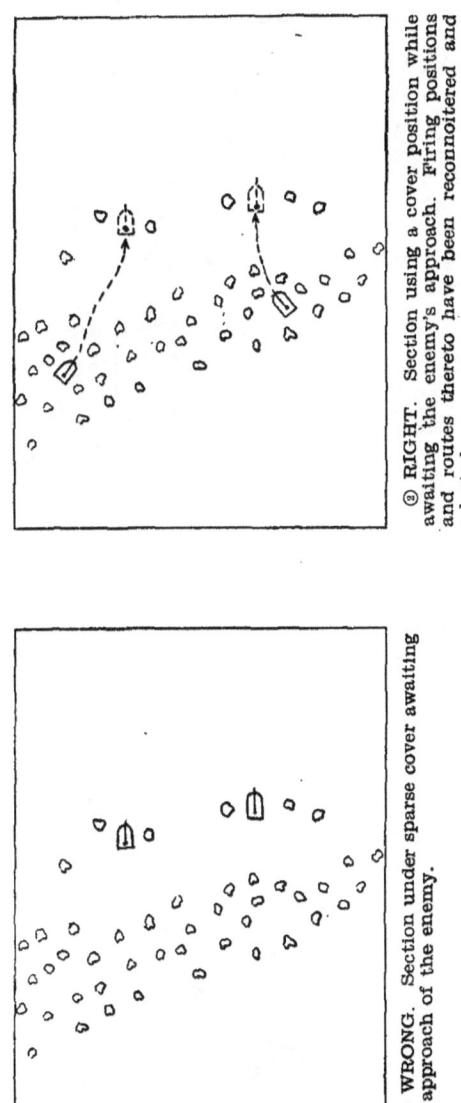

② RIGHT. Section using a cover position while awaiting the enemy's approach. Firing positions and routes thereto have been reconnoitered and selected.

① WRONG. Section under sparse cover awaiting the approach of the enemy.

FIGURE 8.—Use of cover while awaiting enemy.

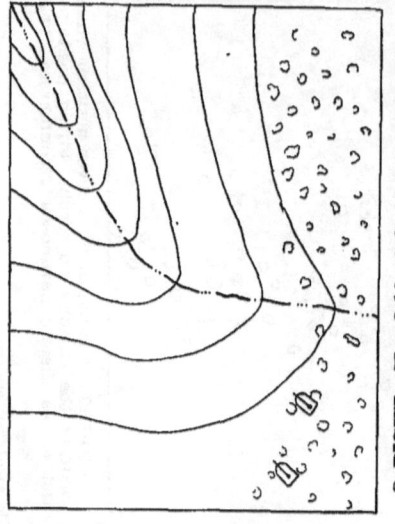

② RIGHT. The field of fire and the ravine are covered from one position. The exact head of the draw, a landmark, is avoided.

FIGURE 9.—Section position.

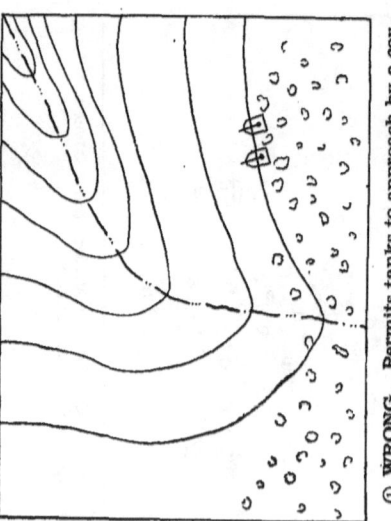

① WRONG. Permits tanks to approach by a covered route, the ravine.

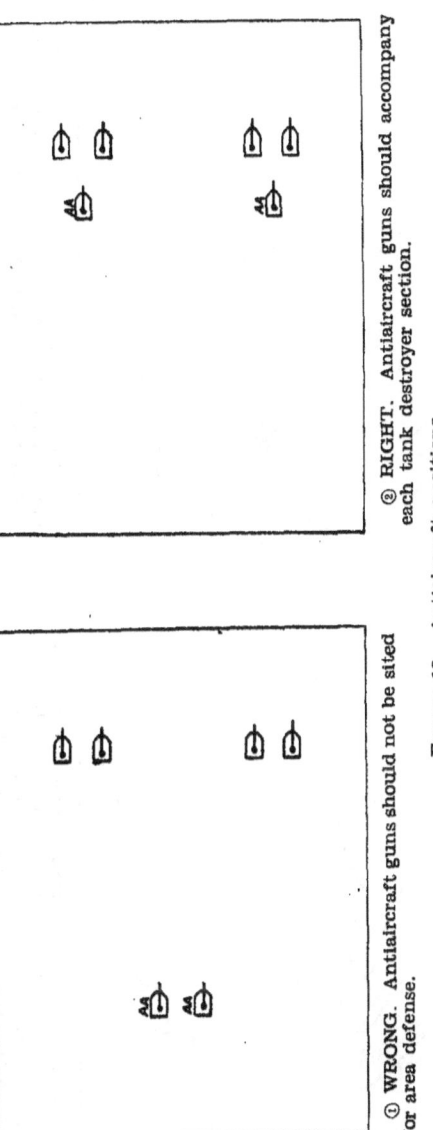

① WRONG. Antiaircraft guns should not be sited for area defense.

② RIGHT. Antiaircraft guns should accompany each tank destroyer section.

FIGURE 10.—Antiaircraft positions.

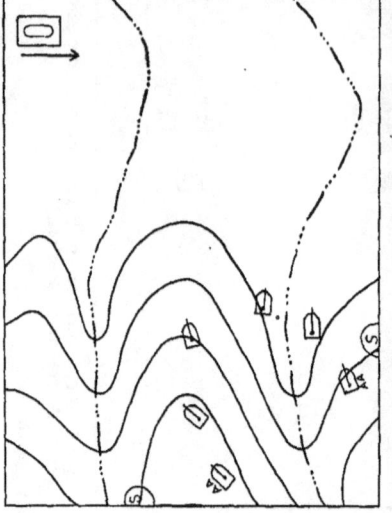

② SOLUTION II. This solution enables the forward guns to fire from a protected position. The rear guns prevent a flanking attack by hostile tanks.

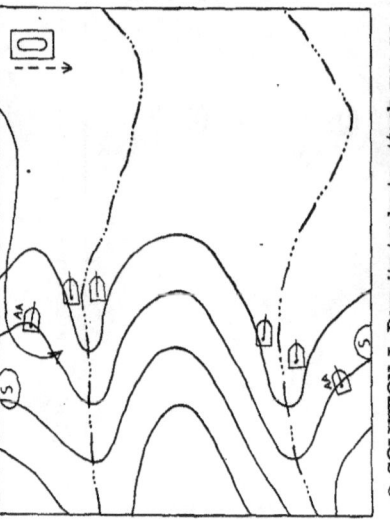

① SOLUTION I. Permits tanks to attack gun positions by a covered route from the rear. It is an excellent position for ambush or if a change to a new position is planned after a few rounds.

FIGURE 11.—Platoon position.

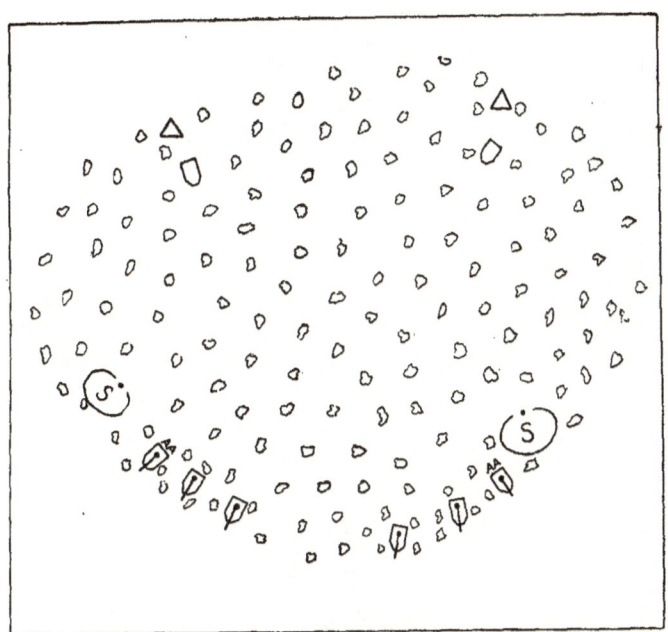

The security section usually takes position in two groups, each group being near a tank destroyer section. Full use should be made of the platoon sergeant's vehicle and the ammunition carrier for obtaining observation; personnel from platoon headquarters can act as observers, the vehicles being parked under nearby cover, prepared to carry a message to the platoon leader by previously selected routes. The antiaircraft guns preferably should be in rear of the tank destroyer guns. However, the necessity for a field of fire against aircraft might cause them to be in position to a flank. The two dispositions of the three guns in line is not desirable but, at times, it cannot be avoided.

FIGURE 12.—Security.

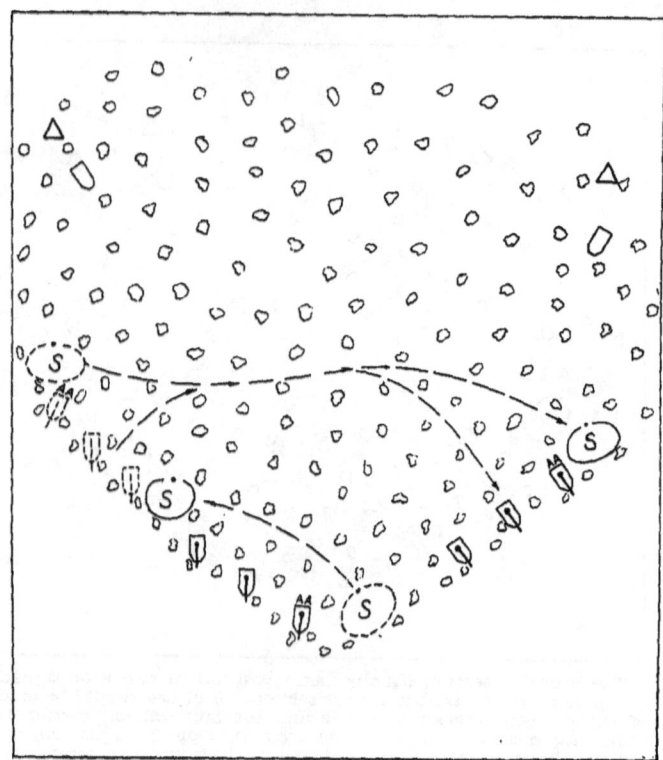

The security group attached to or supporting a tank destroyer
section usually accompanies the section when positions are changed.
Short changes of tank destroyer position ordinarily will not require
a movement by the security squad. The movement of the tank
destroyer section and its attached security group caused the right
flank to be exposed; the other security group moved to cover this
flank.

FIGURE 13.—Security.

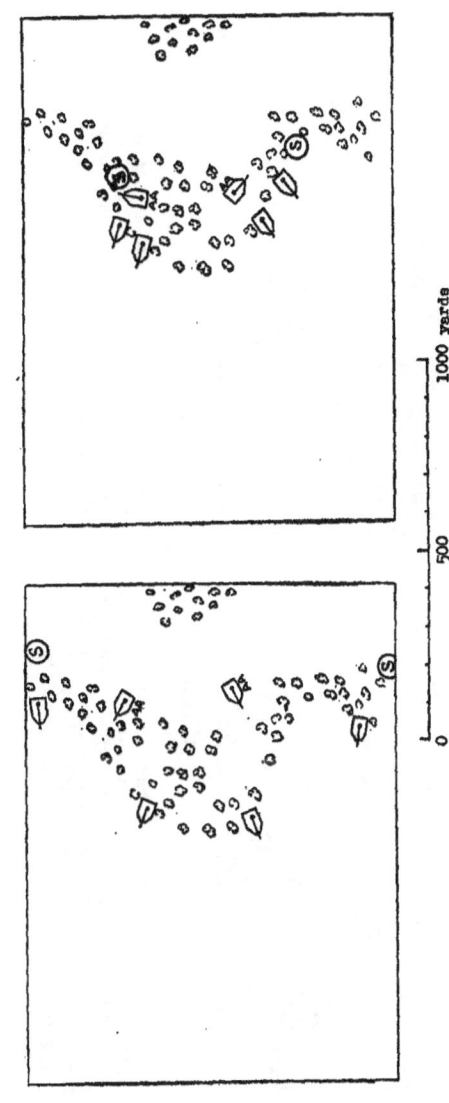

1000 yards

500

0

① WRONG. The excessive separation of the two guns of each section prevents good control; the antiaircraft section cannot effectively protect the flank destroyer guns.

② RIGHT. Grouping permits better control; both sections are covered by the antiaircraft guns.

FIGURE 14.—Platoon position.

154

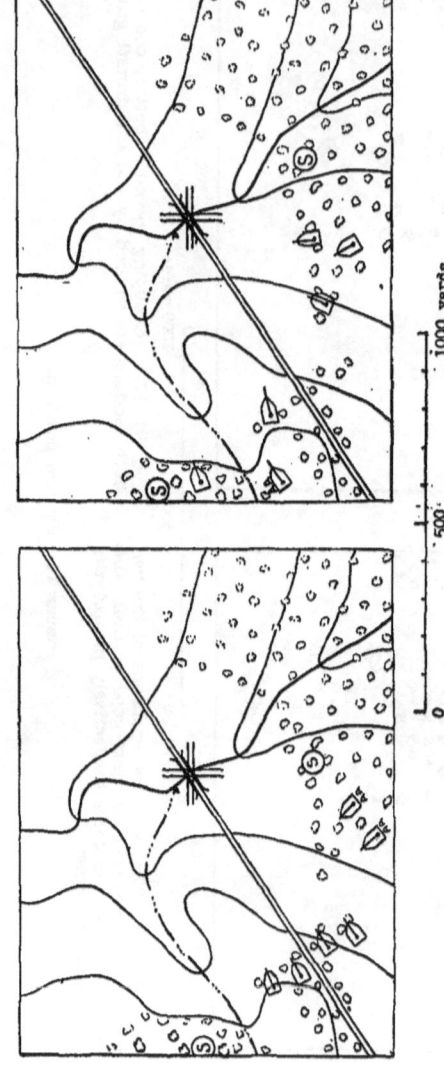

① WRONG. Six errors of guns in a road block position: (1) failure to cover a route of approach, the intermittent stream bed; (2) guns massed; (3) guns at point where road enters woods which is likely to be bombed or interdicted by artillery; (4) guns at point easily seen by hostile patrols; (5) guns in line; (6) antiaircraft guns too distant for effective protection.

② RIGHT. Proper covering of the route of approach; dispersal and echeloning of guns; avoidance of landmark; and effective positioning of antiaircraft guns.

FIGURE 15.—Road block position.

155

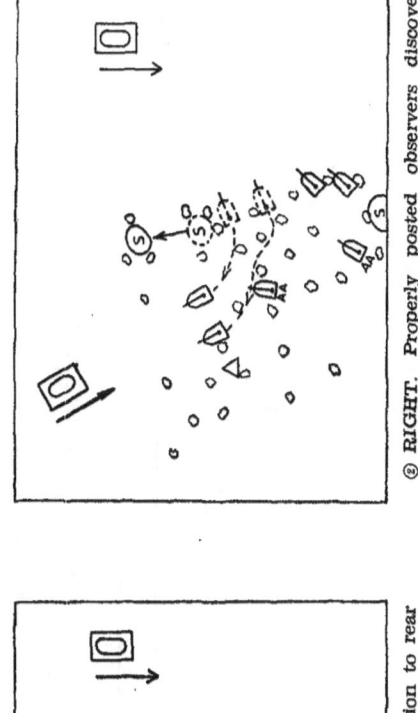

① WRONG. Failure to post observation to rear permits unobserved approach of tanks through the sparse woods.

② RIGHT. Properly posted observers discover the approach of tanks from the rear in time to shift for meeting the new threat.

FIGURE 16.—Platoon security.

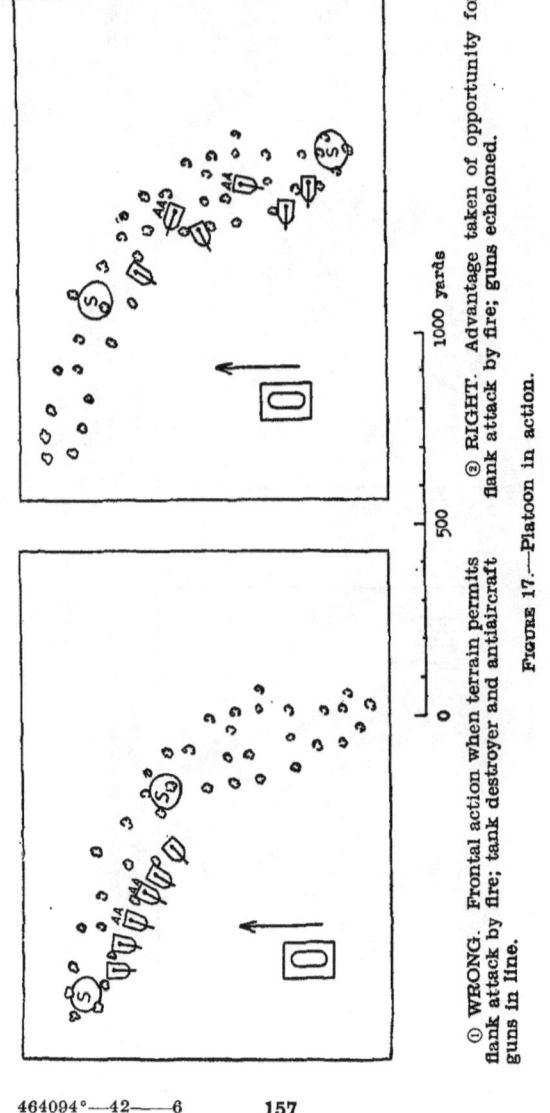

0   500   1000 yards

① WRONG. Frontal action when terrain permits flank attack by fire; tank destroyer and antiaircraft guns in line.

② RIGHT. Advantage taken of opportunity for flank attack by fire; guns echeloned.

FIGURE 17.—Platoon in action.

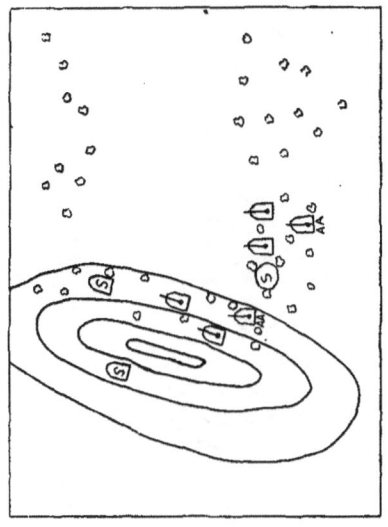

② RIGHT. Section advancing under cover, well protected to the front and to the flanks by security elements.

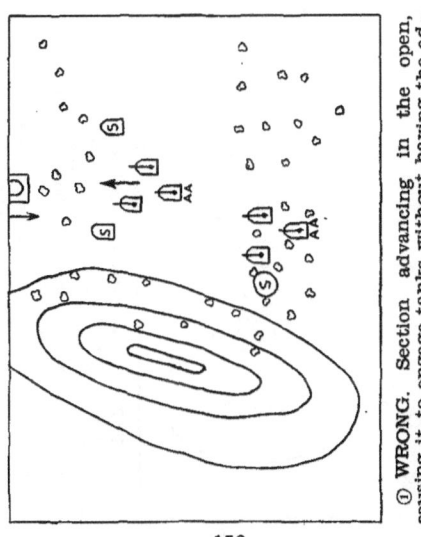

① WRONG. Section advancing in the open, causing it to engage tanks without having the advantage of cover.

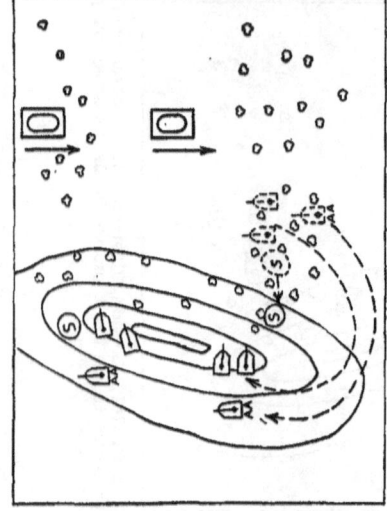

② RIGHT. The security element warns the rest of the advancing section of the approach of hostile tanks. The two tank destroyer guns move by a covered route to a hull defilade position; the antiaircraft squad moves to their rear and takes a position from which fire can be brought against aircraft or against ground targets approaching from the section's left; the security element takes position on the flank.

③ RIGHT. The covering section receives heavy fire. It moves by a covered route to an alternate position and continues the action. The antiaircraft guns remain in readiness; should the tanks come within effective range of the antiaircraft guns, they should join in the fire fight.

FIGURE 18.—Platoon in meeting engagement.

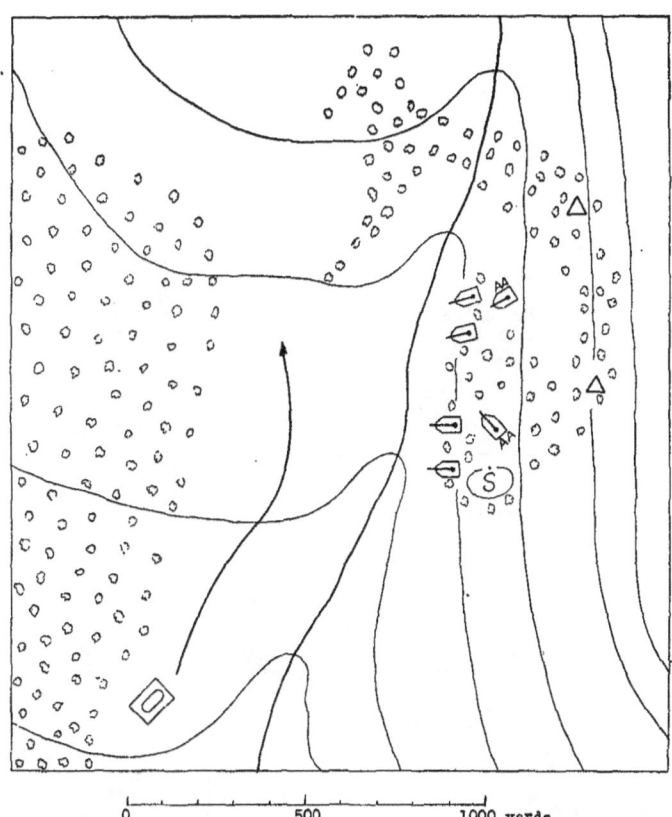

0   500   1000 yards

An example of an excellent position for meeting a tank attack or for attacking tanks by fire from the flank. This position provides a good field of fire, cover, depth, mutual support, an obstacle between the tanks and the tank destroyer guns, covered routes for movement to alternate and supplementary positions, commanding ground for the antiaircraft section, and covered routes for its movement to positions suitable for fire against tanks.

FIGURE 19.—Platoon position.

160

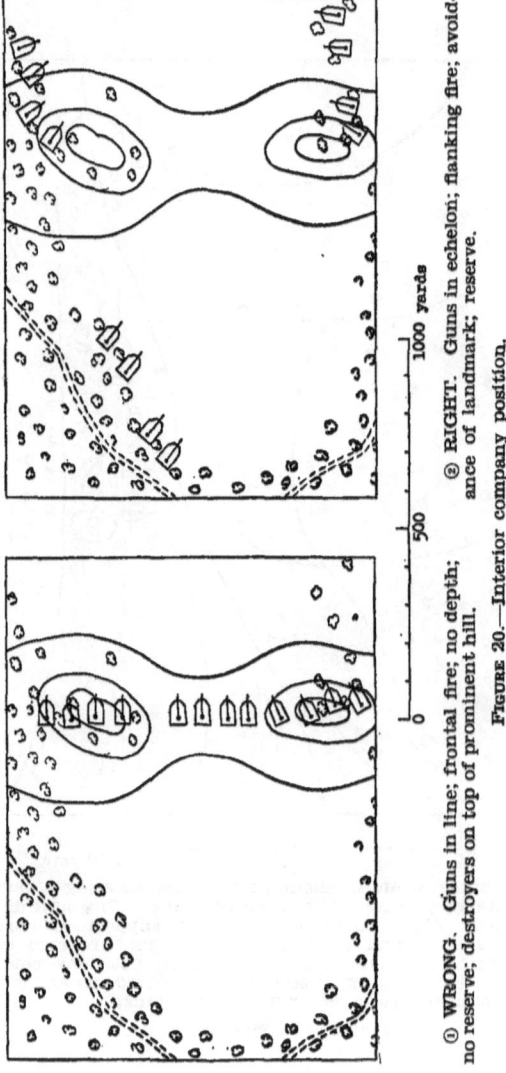

1000 yards

500

0

① WRONG. Guns in line; frontal fire; no depth; no reserve; destroyers on top of prominent hill.

② RIGHT. Guns in echelon; flanking fire; avoidance of landmark; reserve.

FIGURE 20.—Interior company position.

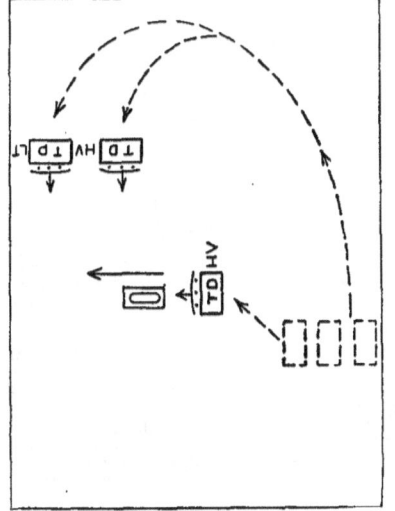

② RIGHT. Direct pressure by a heavy platoon; enveloping or encircling pursuit by the other two platoons, the light platoon leading.

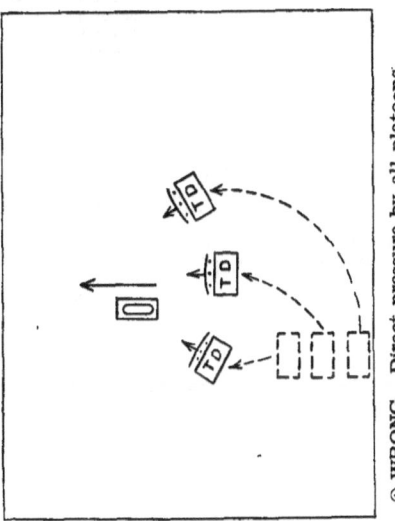

① WRONG. Direct pressure by all platoons.

FIGURE 21.—Company in pursuit (diagrammatic).

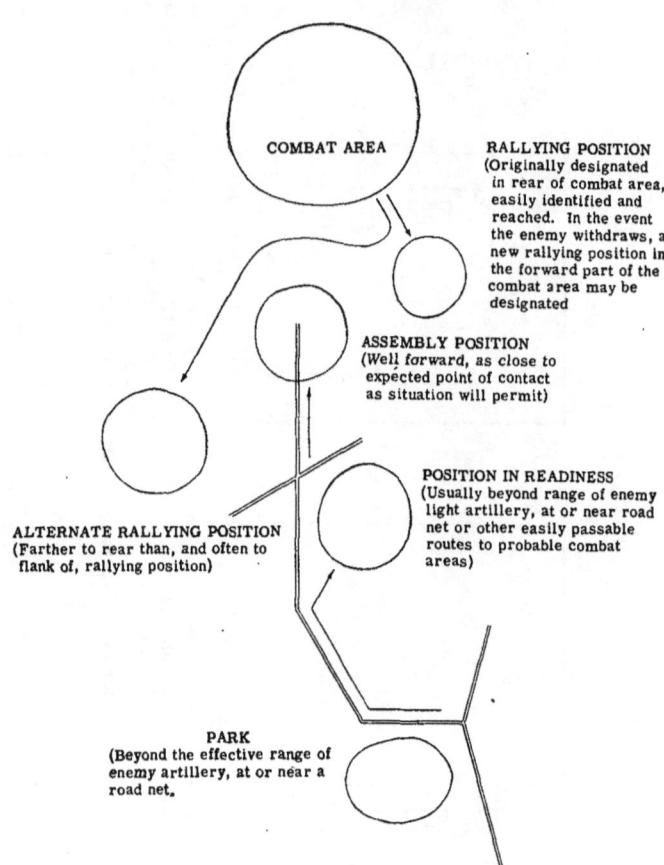

COMBAT AREA

RALLYING POSITION
(Originally designated
in rear of combat area,
easily identified and
reached. In the event
the enemy withdraws, a
new rallying position in
the forward part of the
combat area may be
designated

ASSEMBLY POSITION
(Well forward, as close to
expected point of contact
as situation will permit)

POSITION IN READINESS
(Usually beyond range of enemy
light artillery, at or near road
net or other easily passable
routes to probable combat
areas)

ALTERNATE RALLYING POSITION
(Farther to rear than, and often to
flank of, rallying position)

PARK
(Beyond the effective range of
enemy artillery, at or near a
road net.

FIGURE 22.—Battalion areas (diagrammatic).

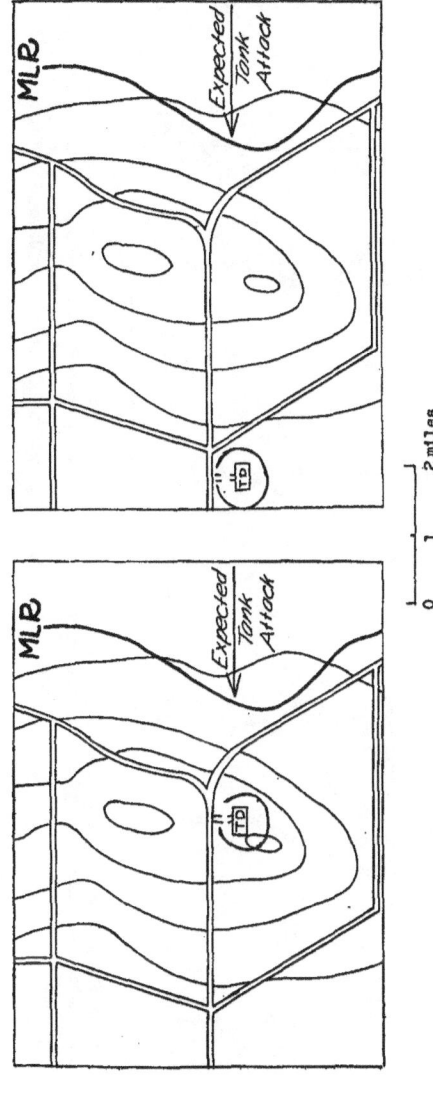

① WRONG. Near main line of resistance, which would result in an exposed lateral movement if enemy attacks to right or left of anticipated point.

② RIGHT. A position which permits the use of covered approaches, including the road net, for lateral movements.

FIGURE 23.—Position in readiness (battalion attached to infantry division).

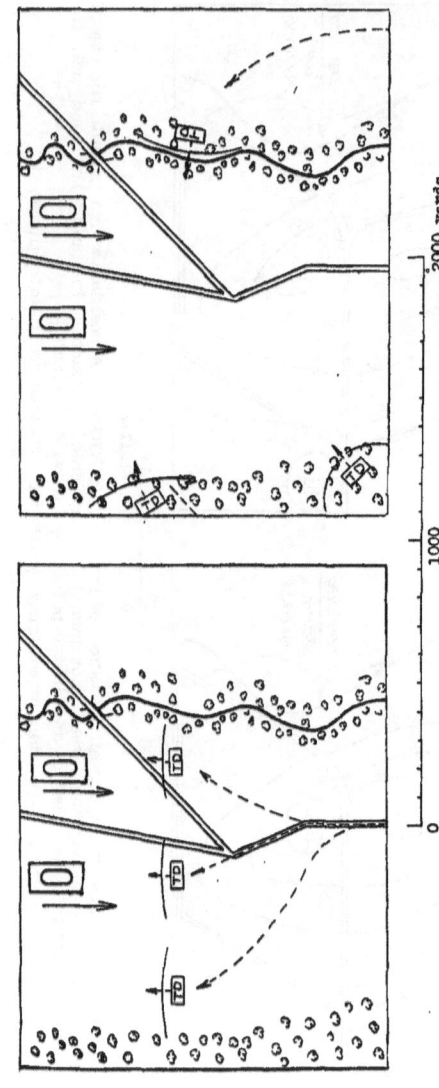

① **WRONG.** Delayed deployment resulting in exposed lateral movement; frontal attack in the open; no reserve.

② **RIGHT.** Prompt deployment; covered flank attacks; reserve. However, fire attacks on both flanks should not be made if they would result in separation of companies beyond effective mutual support.

FIGURE 24.—Battalion in action (reconnaissance company not shown).

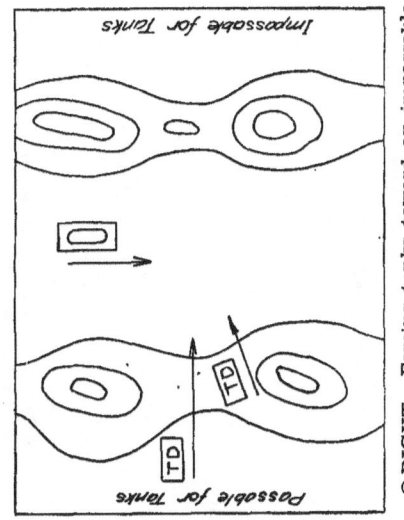

② RIGHT. Forcing tanks toward an impassable area.

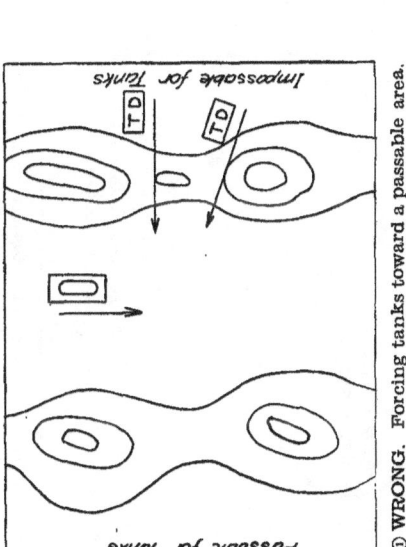

① WRONG. Forcing tanks toward a passable area.

FIGURE 25.—Battalion or group in action (diagrammatic).

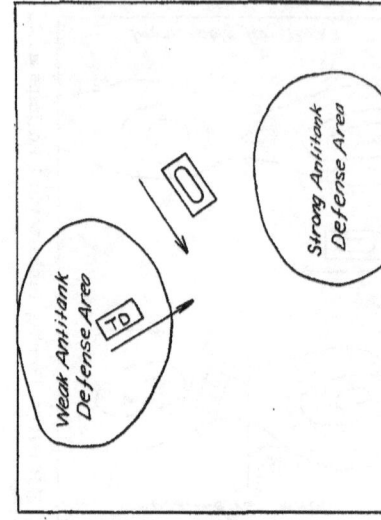

② RIGHT. Forcing tanks toward an area that presents a strong antitank defense.

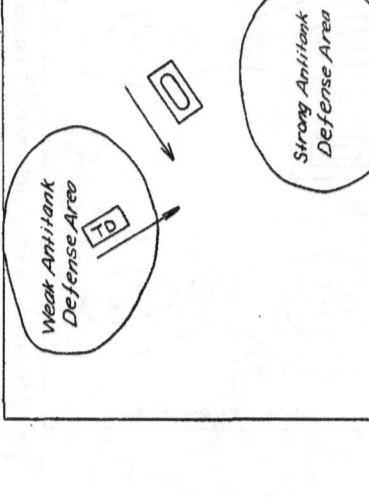

① WRONG. Forcing tanks toward an area that is weakly defended with antitank guns, mines, or other obstacles.

FIGURE 26.—Battalion or group in action (diagrammatic).

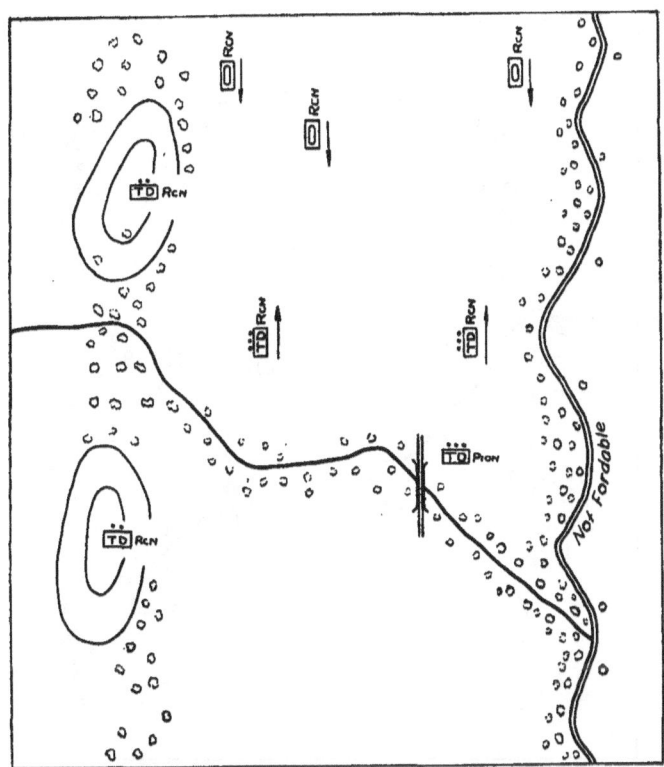

① The reconnaissance company meets reconnaissance elements
of the hostile armored force. Using the minimum of fire and the
maximum of movement, the company locates the hostile flanks
and attempts to determine the enemy's strength and composition.
The pioneer platoon, in anticipation of a possible withdrawal by
the reconnaissance company, prepares to demolish the bridge.

FIGURE 27.—Battalion in action (diagrammatic).

168

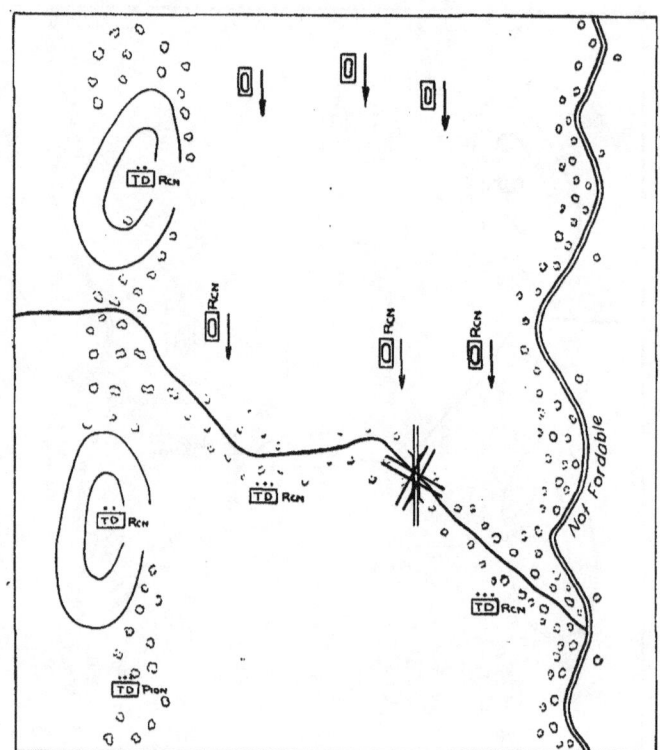

② The reconnaissance company is unable to drive back or penetrate the hostile reconnaissance elements. One reconnaissance platoon remains in observation on the high ground; two platoons maintain contact with, and offer delaying resistance against, the leading hostile elements. The pioneer platoon executes the prepared demolition and moves to a reserve position in the woods.

FIGURE 27—Continued.

169

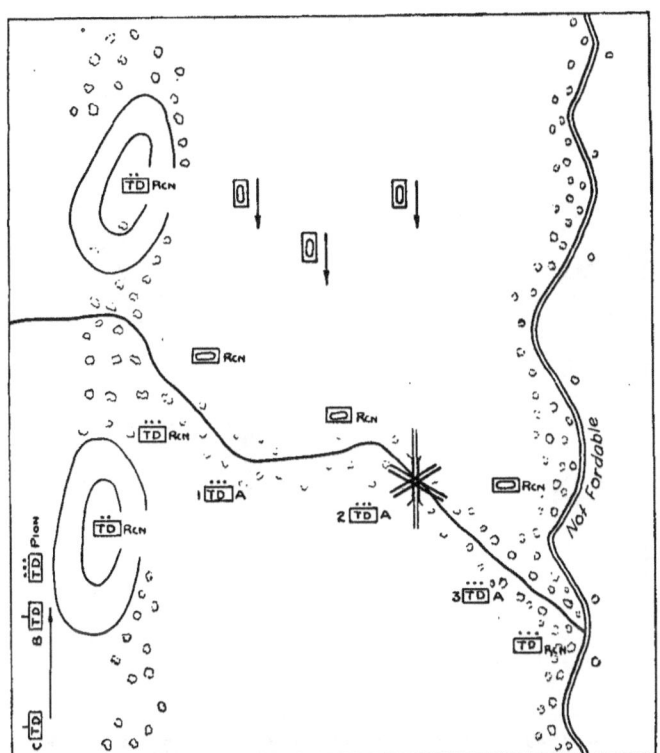

③ One tank destroyer company, Company A, stops the hostile reconnaissance elements behind the obstacle; the two reconnaissance platoons move outward to protect its flanks. The other two tank destroyer companies, Companies B and C, preceded by the pioneer platoon, move toward firing positions.

FIGURE 27—Continued.

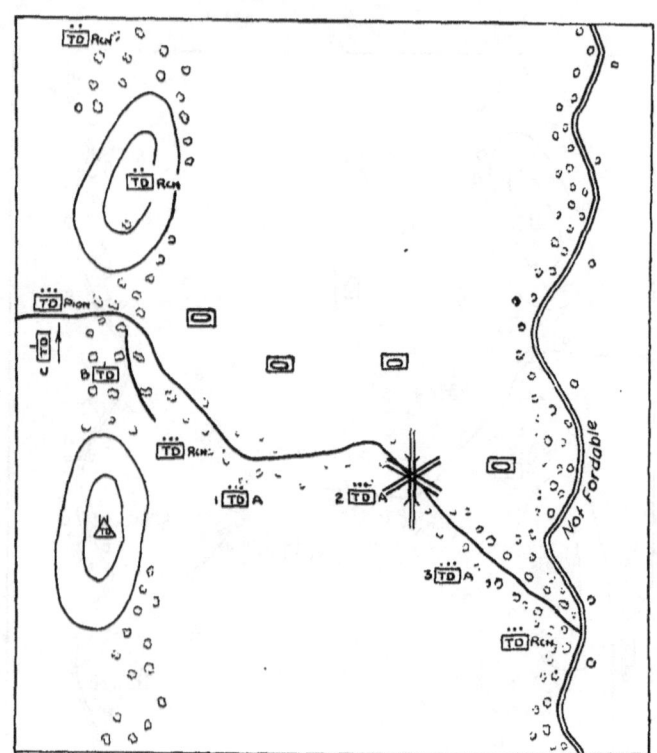

④ Company A remains in position behind the obstacle; guns, sections, and platoons frequently change firing positions. Company B moves to a covered firing position and attacks by fire. The pioneer platoon assists Company C to cross the stream. One reconnaissance section that was observing from the high ground moves to cover a flank. The battalion commander moves to high ground from which he can observe the action.

FIGURE 27—Continued.

171

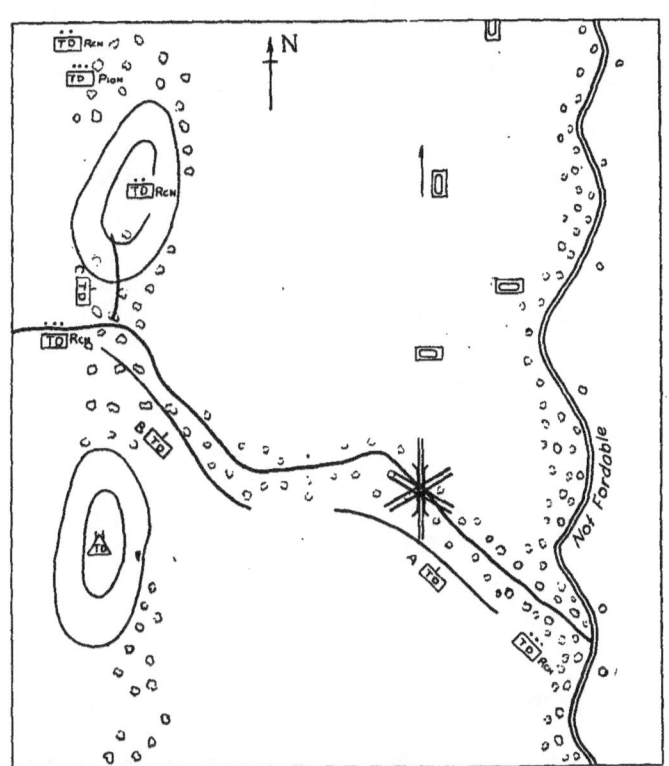

⑥ Company C moves into a covered fire position and the fire of Companies B and C force the tanks to the east. The three platoons of Company A move sucessively under cover to the east and Company B extends in the same direction. The enemy starts to withdraw.

FIGURE 27—Continued.

172

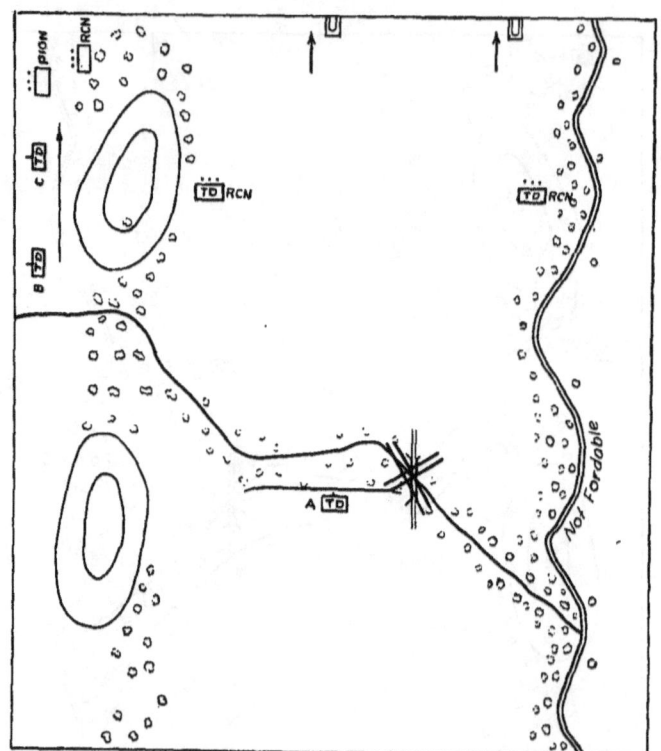

⑥ The enemy withdraws. Two platoons of the reconnaissance company maintain contact with the flanks of the withdrawing force. Company A pursues by direct pressure, using fire and movement but avoiding being caught in the open by any tanks that might turn to face them. Preceded by a reconnaissance and the pioneer platoon, Companies C and B start pursuit by envelopment or encirclement, searching for favorable terrain that can be occupied quickly and which affords good fields of fire.

FIGURE 27—Continued.

173

APPENDIX II

GLOSSARY

Accompanying artillery.—Single batteries, platoons, or pieces attached to assault infantry regiments or battalions for their close support.

Action.—An engagement or battle, usually one on a small scale.

Advance by bounds.—An advance controlled by the assignment of successive movement objectives usually from one terrain line to the next.

Advance by echelon.—An advance of a unit by successive movements of its component elements.

Advance guard.—A security detachment which precedes the main body on the march.

Advance party.—A detachment that is sent out by and moves ahead of the support of the advance guard and forms a reconnoitering element of the support. A detachment which precedes its unit to make administrative or other arrangements.

Aerial (or air) observation.—Observation from balloons, airplanes, or airships.

Air-borne troops.—A general term used to include both parachute and air landing troops.

Alert.—A state of readiness for movement or action. An alarm warning. Vigilant.

Alternate firing position.—A firing position from which the same fire missions can be executed as from the primary firing position.

Ambush.—A concealed place or station where troops lie hidden for the purpose of attacking by surprise. Troops posted in such a position. To attack from such a position.

Approach march.—The advance, usually in extended dispositions from the point where hostile medium artillery fire is expected or air attack is encountered to the point of effective hostile small-arms fire. It ordinarily commences with the development of companies and larger units and termi-

174

nates with their complete or partial deployment as skirmishers.

Assembly area (or position).——The area in which elements of a command are organized preparatory to further action. For example, in the attack, liaison with supporting arms is arranged; objectives and other missions are assigned to component units.

Axial road.—A road along the contemplated direction of advance.

Bivouac.—An area in which troops rest on the ground with no overhead cover or under natural cover, shelter tents, or improvised shelter.

Bridgehead.—Position occupied by advance troops to protect the passage of a river or defile by the remainder of the command.

Canalize.—To restrict an advance by natural or artificial obstacles and by fire into a narrow zone.

Clear (in the).—The sending of messages, orders, or instructions in plain (uncoded) language.

Clear (verb).—To pass a designated point or line. Refers to the tail of a unit.

Combat echelon.—The principal element of offensive or defensive power, for example, the infantry echelon in defense occupying the principal battle position.

Combat vehicle.—A self-propelled, armed vehicle, with or without armor, manned by combat personnel.

Compartments of terrain.—An area of terrain inclosed on at least two sides by critical terrain features such as ridge lines, woods, or water courses.

Convoy.—Any group of transportation temporarily organized to operate as a unit during movement. To escort. To accompany for the purpose of protecting.

Corridor.—A compartment of terrain of which the longer dimension lies generally in the direction of movement or leads toward an objective. For example, an avenue of approach having natural terrain features on its two flanks which limit observation and direct fire from positions outside the corridor constitutes favorable lines of advance for friendly or hostile forces.

175

Counterattack.—An attack by part or all of the defending force against a hostile attacking force for the purpose of regaining ground lost or for destroying hostile elements.

Counterreconnaissance.—Measures taken to screen a command from hostile ground and air observation and reconnaissance.

Cover.—Natural or artificial shelter or protection from fire or observation, or any object affording such protection. The vertical relief of a trench measured from the bottom, or from the trench board, to the top of the parapet. To protect or provide security for another force or a locality.

Defiladed.—Protected from hostile ground observation and fire by a mask.

Delaying action.—A form of defensive action employed to slow up the enemy's advance and gain time without becoming decisively engaged.

Development.—The distribution of a command from mass or route-column dispositions into smaller columns or groups in preparation for action. The extension in width and depth of companies and larger units preparatory to approach march.

Direct fire.—Fire in which the firer aims the weapon by means of sights directly at the target.

Displacement.—The movement of supporting weapons from one firing position area to another, for example, in attack the successive movement of supporting weapons to correspond with the progress of the attacking echelon in order to keep weapons within efficient supporting distance thereof.

Element.—One of the subdivisions of a command. The term "elements" is used in an inclusive sense to refer to all those various smaller units or parts of units, generally different in character; as *service elements*, meaning quartermaster, ordnance, engineer, and medical units, etc.

Emplacement.—A prepared position from which a unit or a weapon executes its fire missions.

Enfilade (verb).—To fire at a target so that the fire coincides with the long axis of the target, for example, to fire against troops disposed in a generally linear formation from their direct flank and along the direction of their front.

176

Envelopment.—An attack against one or both hostile flanks, usually assisted by a secondary attack against the enemy's front.

Flank.—The side of a command from the leading to the rearmost element, inclusive. *Right* flank is the right side when facing the enemy, and does not change when the command is moving to the rear.

Holding attack (secondary attack).—The part of the attack designed to hold the enemy in position and prevent the redistribution of his reserves; it is ordinarily directed against the hostile front.

Hull defilade (or hull down).—Position taken by destroyer which provides defilade for the hull of the vehicle.

Infiltrate.—To pass troops in relatively small numbers through gaps in the enemy position or his field of fire, for example, to advance individuals by bounds during an attack.

Liaison.—The connection established between units or elements by a representative, usually an officer, of one unit who visits or remains with another unit.

Lightly armored vehicle.—An armored vehicle which provides armor protection from small arms fire for its crew and/or engine.

Local security.—A security element, independent or an outpost, established by a subordinate commander to protect his unit against surprise and to insure its readiness for action.

Logistics.—That branch of military art that comprises everything relating to movement, supply, and evacuation.

Main attack.—That part of the attack where the commander concentrates the greatest possible power. *Compare* Holding attack.

March unit.—A subdivision of a marching column which moves and halts at the command or signal of its commander.

Mask (obstruction).—Any natural or artificial obstruction which interferes with view of fire, usually an intervening hill, woods, etc. Friendly troops located between a gun and its target may constitute a mask.

177

Motorized unit.—A unit equipped either organically or temporarily with sufficient motor vehicles to carry all its matériel and personnel at the same time.

Mutual support.—The support involving fire or movement or both, rendered one another by adjacent elements.

Normal impact.—The impact of a projectile against a surface in which the line of flight of the projectile is perpendicular to the surface struck.

Organization. (*See* Unit.)

Park.—An area used for the purpose of servicing, maintaining, and parking vehicles.

.*Penetration.*—A form of attack in which the main attack seeks to break the continuity of the enemy's front and to envelop the flanks thus created.

Phase line.—A line or terrain feature on which units may be halted for control, coordination, or further orders.

Point.—The patrol or reconnaissance element which precedes the advance party of an advance guard, or follows the rear party of a rear guard.

Position in readiness.—A position assumed as a temporary expedient in a situation so clouded with uncertainty that positive action is considered unwarranted.

Rate of march.—The average speed over a period of time including short periodic halts.

Rear guard.—A security detachment which follows the main body and protects it on the march.

Rear party.—The detachment from the support of a rear guard which follows and protects it on the march.

Reconnaissance.—The operation of searching for information in the field.

Reserve.—A fraction of a command held initially under the control of the commander to influence future action.

Retreat.—An involuntary retrograde movement forced on a command as a result of an unsuccessful operation or combat. The act of retreating. To retire from any position or place. To withdraw.

Retrograde movement.—A movement to the rear.

Road block.—A barrier to block or limit the movement of hostile vehicles along a road.

Road space.—The distance from head to tail of a column when it is in a prescribed formation on a road.

Screen.—To prevent hostile ground reconnaissance or observation. The body of troops used to screen a command.

Screening smoke.—A chemical agent used to blind hostile observation.

Sector.—The defense area designated by boundaries within which a unit operates on the defense.

Signal operation instructions (SOI).—A type of combat orders issued for the technical control and coordination of signal agencies throughout the command.

Slit trench.—A very narrow trench used for protection against shell fire and passage of tanks, especially in massing troops close to the front.

Speed.—The rapidity of movement at any particular instant expressed in miles per hour.

Standing operating procedure (SOP).—Routine procedure prescribed to be carried out in the absence of orders to the contrary.

Support (of advance guard).—The echelon of the advance guard that precedes the advance-guard reserve. The support sends out, and is preceded by, the advance party.

Supporting fire.—Fire delivered by auxiliary weapons on the immediate objectives of attacking elements.

Surveillance.—An active, thorough, and continuous search by observation and reconnaissance of an area or of hostile dispositions.

Task force.—A temporary tactical unit, composed of elements of one or more arms and services, formed for the execution of a specific mission or operation.

Unit.—A military force having a prescribed organization.

Unit of fire.—The quantity in rounds or tons of ammunition, bombs, grenades, and pyrotechnics which a designated organization or weapon may be expected to expend on the average in one day of combat.

Warning order.—An order issued as a preliminary to another order, especially for a movement, which is to follow; it may be a message or a field order, and may be either written, dictated, or oral. The purpose is to give advance information so that the commanders may make necessary arrangements to facilitate the execution of the subsequent field order.

Wave.—One of a series of lines of forages, mechanized vehicles, skirmishers, or small columns into which an attack unit is deployed in depth.

Zone of action.—A zone designated by boundaries in an advance or a retrograde movement within which the unit operates.

NOTE.—Additional military terms applicable to operations of armored forces are contained in FM 17–10 and other manuals.

INDEX

www.ingramcontent.com/pod-product-compliance
Lightning Source LLC
Chambersburg PA
CBHW021603280526
45784CB00001BA/482